FOREWORD

Over the past three years the Government have published a series of consultants' reports examining factors relevant to the application of market-based instruments to waste management polices; especially as these relate to the landfilling of waste.

This latest study provides an analysis of the best available evidence available as to the sources by main industrial group of waste arisings which are landfilled in the UK. Future trends in industrial waste production and information on waste composition and on disposal costs are also examined. The study's findings reflect the uncertainty which remains over the sources of such wastes. This is an issue which the recently published draft "Waste Strategy for England and Wales" highlights and which is being addressed by the information strategy described in that document.

Nevertheless, the results provided here are a useful guide to those industrial groups most likely to be affected by the higher waste disposal costs resulting from influences such as the introduction of higher environmental standards for landfill; market pressures; and the introduction of the landfill tax which was announced in the Budget in November 1994.

Department of the Environment   March 1995

5

Department of the Environment

ANALYSIS OF INDUSTRIAL AND COMMERCIAL WASTE GOING TO LANDFILL IN THE UK

A Study by M.E.L Research

LONDON: HMSO

ISBN 0 11 753066 2

PREFACE

M.E.L Research was commissioned in February 1994 by the Department of the Environment to carry out a brief review of available data on the quantity, composition and costs of disposal of controlled industrial and commercial waste going to landfill in the UK and to provide best estimates of those data which might be used to inform future waste management policy.

There is currently no published or publicly available information on the quantities of waste being landfilled in the UK according to the industry group of origin. This information is central to consideration of the wider costs to industry of any policy which affects the price of landfill. We have therefore had to compile disparate pieces of data to arrive at a best estimate. It has to be borne in mind that any information not based on weighing waste and surveying every company in the UK is prone to errors; the data presented in this report must be viewed as best estimates of the actual quantities of waste being landfilled in the UK.

M.E.L Research would like to thank all the organisations which kindly agreed for their data to be used in this project. We would like to pay recognition to the advice and assistance provided by all members of the steering group consisting of officials from the Department of the Environment and the Department of Trade and Industry and the particular contributions made by Bob Davies, the Nominated Officer, and Dr Christine Ogden. In addition, many organisations provided data and advice and particular mention should go to Steve Webb at NAWDC, CIRIA, the British Scrap Federation and the Institute of Grocery Distribution. We are especially grateful to West Midlands Waste Management Coordinating Authority, Humberside Waste Regulation Authority and Norfolk County Council for allowing us to use their survey data. Nevertheless, the views expressed in this report are those of M.E.L Research and may not reflect those held by any other organisation.

Research Team:

Barbara Leach BA
Principal Investigator, supported by:

Phil Edwards BSc CStat
Sharan Gill BSc
Rob Pocock BSc PhD MIWM

Waste Management Research Unit
M.E.L Research Report 9402/1

CONTENTS

EXECUTIVE SUMMARY

Background to the Study

E.1   M.E.L Research was commissioned in February 1994 by the Department of the Environment to carry out a brief review of available data on the quantity, composition and costs of disposal of controlled industrial and commercial waste going to landfill in the UK and to provide best estimates of those data which might be used to inform future waste management policy.

Overview of the Approach to the Study

E.2   There is no information directly available on the quantities and types of industrial and commercial waste being **landfilled** in the UK according to industry of origin. However, there is information that can be used to estimate the quantity and composition of waste **arising** within each sector of industry and commerce and there is also limited information on the quantity and type of waste being landfilled although not by industry of origin.

E.3   There are therefore two approaches to estimating the quantity and type of waste being landfilled:

1.   Use available data on waste arisings by industry sector and apply a factor to each to estimate the proportion being landfilled

2.   Use available data on waste disposals and try to work backwards to determine the likely industries of origin.

E.4   As in this project it is the industry of origin that is most important for assessing the likely costs to be incurred if a fiscal instrument based on tonnages of waste being landfilled were to be introduced, it was decided that the former method would be used, cross-referring to the second set of data in order to be confident that estimates are of the correct order of magnitude. This method is likely to produce the most accurate breakdown of waste attributable to the various sectors of industry and commerce.

Overview of the Methodology

E.5   Given the lack of any single central information source, we have had to compile disparate pieces of data to arrive at a best estimate of the distribution by industry of origin of landfilled waste. The broad method adopted was as follows.

1. Produce estimates of controlled industrial and commercial waste arising in the UK by industry of origin.

2. Produce estimates of the proportion of this being landfilled in the UK by industry of origin.

3. Produce a grouped industry classification based on Standard Industrial Classification 1980.

4. Provide estimates, by industry sector, of the total annual cost of a notional £5 increase in the price of landfilling waste and show these as a percentage of the relevant sector's annual gross output.

5. Provide an indication of the composition of this waste.

6. Provide an indication of likely future trends in waste generation and hence the future distribution of additional costs to industry.

Sources of Error

E.6 Various kinds of error will be present in the data used for this project. In addition, various assumptions have had to be made during the estimation procedure. Perhaps the most significant of these is the assumption that waste is generated proportional to the number of people employed on a premises. Some assumption along these lines is necessary both to fill in gaps left by missing data and to forecast future waste arisings.

E.7 There is a long-standing debate about the merits of this method. We recognise that there are likely to be inaccuracies involved in using this method but in the absence of data on other proxy variables such as output, energy usage, floor space, gross value added and rateable value, and without research to determine which are the best to use, the use of employment data has had to be regarded as the best method available. In addition, other assumptions have had to be made in converting data in 1968 Standard Industrial Classification (SIC) format to 1980 SIC format and in disaggregating from SIC Division to SIC Class.

E.8 It has to be borne in mind that any information not based on weighing waste and surveying every company in the UK is prone to errors; the data presented in this report must be viewed as best estimates of actual quantities of waste being landfilled in the UK.

ESTIMATING WASTE ARISINGS

E.9 There are three main sources of data on waste arising in the UK:

1. **Estimates published in Waste Disposal Plans**
2. **Raw survey data from Waste Regulation Authorities**
3. Other published survey results

E.10 Data published in 27 English Waste Disposal Plans were used to estimate waste arisings by industry group for the whole of the UK by using employment data to provide an estimate where Disposal Plan data were missing.

E.11 Raw data from four surveys of individual commercial and industrial premises were also used as an alternative source of information to provide an estimate of industrial and commercial waste arising in the UK. This approach involves using a minimum variance unbiased estimate of the average tonnes of waste per employee coefficient for each industry group to determine arisings for the whole of the UK. Although the coefficients are based on data from only four areas, for the majority of industry sectors there is no statistical evidence to show that the average waste per employee coefficients differ significantly amongst the four areas surveyed. Despite small sample sizes in several industry sectors, the variance of the estimated mean is relatively small; the small samples in these sectors reflect the fact that there are few businesses within them in the UK as a whole.

E.12 It should be noted that the base data for both the Waste Disposal Plans and the Waste Regulation Authorities' surveys were only available for areas of England. UK estimates have been extrapolated from these data using numbers of employees. The implied estimates for Northern Ireland, Scotland and Wales should not be treated as having any separate validity but rather as a means of arriving at a UK estimate. However, the estimate for Scotland of 11 million tonnes arising is of a similar order of magnitude to that published in the Hazardous Waste Inspectorate Scotland Report (1991/2) which cites provisional arisings figures of 1.5 million tonnes of commercial waste and 8.4 million tonnes of industrial waste, a total of around 10 million tonnes.

E.13 The results of two surveys conducted by Warren Spring Laboratory have been included for comparative purposes only as the total arisings figures were considerably lower than other published data. In addition, results of surveys conducted in The Netherlands and Germany have been included, again for comparative purposes as it is difficult to determine whether observed differences in quantities of waste generated per employee are 'real' or simply reflect different methodologies employed.

ESTIMATING WASTE BEING LANDFILLED

E.14 There is very little information on the extent to which the various disposal routes for industrial, commercial and construction waste are utilised and, in particular, on the proportion of waste going to landfill sites by the industry of origin. The recently published research report *Externalities From Landfill and Incineration* (CSERGE, WSL and EFTEL) shows estimates of the proportion of waste going to landfill by broad industrial groupings (industrial, commercial and construction). These figures have been used to convert waste arisings estimates from the Waste Regulation Authorities' surveys and the Waste Disposal Plans into amounts of waste landfilled. There are no data on the proportion of waste going to landfill sites by the industry of origin in any more detail than those broad groupings referred to above.

E.15 Two independent estimates for individual industrial sectors have been used to refine these base data. Firstly, as part of a larger study of construction and demolition waste in the UK, Howard Humphreys consultants conducted a survey of waste currently going to landfill. Their estimate of about 40 million tonnes a year, which is the figure used in the recently published consultation draft of A Waste Strategy for England and Wales (DoE 1995), is very much higher than the previously published figure (13 million tonnes), the Waste Disposal Plan estimate (11 million tonnes) or the survey-derived estimate (2 million tonnes). Howard Humphreys acknowledge that their estimate is likely to be on the high side. For instance, excluding 'hard materials' of the sort used to assist in the engineering of sites would reduce their figure to about 30 million tonnes a year. After careful consideration of all the available evidence, it has been decided to include the Waste Disposal Plan figure of 11 million tonnes in the survey as well as the Waste Disposal Plan distributions. It should be easier to assess the status of the Howard Humphreys estimate once their research report has been published and comments on it received.

E.16 Secondly, information supplied directly by the British Scrap Federation has been used to derive the quantity of waste from dealers in scrap and waste materials (SIC Class 62) going to landfill.

E.17 Table E.1 shows the estimated distribution by industry of the amount of waste going to landfill per annum using both the Waste Disposal Plan and the survey data sources together with a comparison between the two sets of figures.

E.18 Both overall estimates (about 73 million tonnes per annum from the survey data and 83 million tonnes from the Waste Disposal Plan data) are broadly consistent with each other and with the most recently published estimate for industrial and commercial waste in *Sustainable Development: The UK Strategy* of about 73 million tonnes. It should be noted, however, that the recent Howard Humphreys' estimate for construction waste would add about 20 million tonnes or more to these totals.

E.19 While the overall totals are consistent with one another, there are large discrepancies between the two estimates within some of the industry groups, notably the chemical industry (SIC Class 25), manufacturing of non-metallic products (SIC Class 24) and metal manufacturing (SIC Class 22). On the whole, the Waste Disposal Plan estimates for industry groups within manufacturing tend to be higher than the survey estimates while the converse is true for the commercial sector. These observations may in part be due to the fact that data from Waste Disposal Plans are less recent than those from the surveys. Over the last fifteen years, the manufacturing sector in the UK as a whole has declined while the service sector has grown and this may explain some of the differences between the estimates. We would tend to favour the use of the survey data partly for the reason outlined above but also since the use of raw data enables the estimation errors to be minimised (through the use of the minimum variance estimate of the mean, for example) and allows confidence limits to be produced.

Table E.1: Estimated UK Waste to Landfill by Industry of Origin per Annum

INDUSTRY GROUP	TONNES OF WASTE LANDFILLED PER ANNUM		DIFFERENCE BETWEEN THE TWO
	Survey data ('000 tonnes)	WDP data ('000 tonnes)	DATA SETS ('000 tonnes)
Coal extraction; coke ovens; extraction of oil and gas etc	896	2,600	-1,704
Prod and dist of electricity, gas and other forms of energy	1,189	3,832	-2,643
Water supply industry	60	949	-888
Extraction and preparation of metalliferous mineral ores	MISSING	MISSING	MISSING
Metal manufacturing	1,701	8,334	-6,634
Extraction of minerals not elsewhere specified	5	1,720	-1,715
Manufacture of non-metallic mineral products	2,101	10,611	-8,509
Chemical industry	2,145	18,771	-16,626
Production of man-made fibres	9	363	-354
Manufacture of metal goods not elsewhere specified	1,910	622	1,288
Mechanical engineering	2,026	1,517	509
Manufacture of office machinery & data processing equip.	8	160	-153
Electrical and electronic engineering	1,284	1,118	166
Manufacture of motor vehicles and parts thereof	1,385	504	881
Manufacture of other transport equipment	681	501	180
Instrument engineering	489	189	300
Food, drink and tobacco manufacturing industries	5,511	1,903	3,608
Textiles, leather and leather goods, footwear and clothing	1,194	1,535	-341
Timber and wooden furniture industries	2,382	751	1,631
Man. of paper and paper products; printing and publishing	1,728	1,629	100
Processing of rubber and plastics	815	727	88
Other manufacturing industries	151	247	-96
Construction	11,872	11,872	n/a
Wholesale distribution	3,752	1,188	2,563
Dealing in scrap and waste materials	500	500	n/a
Commission agents	MISSING	44	MISSING
Retail distribution	9,163	3,133	6,030
Hotels and catering	3,291	1,614	1,678
Repair of consumer goods and vehicles	332	259	74
Transport and communication	2,548	1,255	1,293
Banking, finance, insurance, business services, leasing	5,096	887	4,209
Other services	8,992	3,930	5,062
All economic activities	73,216	83,265	-10,049

Negative numbers in the right hand column indicate that the Waste Disposal Plan data are greater than the survey data

POSSIBLE IMPACT ON INDUSTRY OF AN INCREASE IN LANDFILL PRICE

E.20 The price of landfill has been projected as being likely to rise significantly over the next few years (see for instance Landfill Costs and Prices: Correcting Possible Market Distortions HMSO 1993). The recent announcement of the introduction of a landfill tax in 1996 will be one of the factors leading to higher landfill prices. In order to illustrate the effects of these trends, a purely notional flat rate increase of £5 per tonne in landfill costs has been applied to the figures in Table E.1 to show the likely impact on the various sectors of industry.

E.21 The results are presented in Table E.2 together with the cost of the increase to be borne by each sector expressed as a percentage of its annual gross output. Figures for gross output have been obtained from the Census of Production and relate to 1991 with the exception of the figure for the construction industry for which data were only available for 1990. As a consequence of using employment as a proxy estimator for waste generation, estimates of waste being landfilled produced from both data sources relate to the year of the employment data, again 1991.

E.22 The estimated total costs to industry and commerce in the UK range between £366 million and £416 million, depending upon which source of data is used to produce the estimates. The relative impact is obviously proportional to the tonnages generated by the various sectors of industry and commerce and this distribution will therefore mirror that discussed in E.17 of this report. The construction industry would experience an additional cost of around £59 million although this could be as high as £129 million if the estimates of waste being landfilled by this industry sector suggested by Howard Humphreys were applied. The costs to the service sector (SIC Classes 61-99) could be as high as £169 million according to estimates produced using the survey data.

E.23 The relative impact of these increased disposal costs expressed as a percentage of annual gross output cannot be determined for the service sector as no suitable information could be found. Table E.2 shows, however, that for the construction industry (SIC Class 50), a £5 increase per tonne of waste landfilled would equate to 0.08% of the annual gross output of that industry or as much as 0.22% according to the estimates produced by Howard Humphreys. For the manufacturing sector (SIC Classes 22-49), the relative impact ranges between around 0.01% of annual gross output to around 1%, the average relative impact being around 0.1%.

E.24 It should be emphasised that all these estimates are based on a notional, flat rate per tonne price increase. A fixed percentage increase in price would produce a different pattern of increases across industrial sectors which would reflect the amount *and relative cost of disposal* for each industry.

Table E.2: Estimated Impact of an Increase in Landfill Costs

INDUSTRY GROUP	COST OF A £5 INCREASE IN LANDFILL PRICE (£ MILLION)		COST OF INCREASE AS % OF OUTPUT	
	Survey data	WDP data	Survey data	WDP data
Coal extraction; coke ovens; extraction of oil and gas etc	4.5	13.0	0.01%	0.04%
Prod and dist of electricity, gas and other forms of energy	5.9	19.2	0.02%	0.05%
Water supply industry	0.3	4.7	0.01%	0.16%
Extraction and preparation of metalliferous mineral ores	MISSING	MISSING	MISSING	MISSING
Metal manufacturing	8.5	41.7	0.07%	0.33%
Extraction of minerals not elsewhere specified	not sig	8.6	not sig	1.23%
Manufacture of non-metallic mineral products	10.5	53.1	0.09%	0.47%
Chemical industry	10.7	93.9	0.03%	0.28%
Production of man-made fibres	not sig	1.8	not sig	0.18%
Manufacture of metal goods not elsewhere specified	9.5	3.1	0.07%	0.02%
Mechanical engineering	10.1	7.6	0.03%	0.02%
Manufacture of office machinery & data processing equip.	not sig	0.8	not sig	0.01%
Electrical and electronic engineering	6.4	5.6	0.02%	0.02%
Manufacture of motor vehicles and parts thereof	6.9	2.5	0.03%	0.01%
Manufacture of other transport equipment	3.4	2.5	0.02%	0.02%
Instrument engineering	2.4	0.9	0.06%	0.02%
Food, drink and tobacco manufacturing industries	27.6	9.5	0.05%	0.02%
Textiles, leather and leather goods, footwear and clothing	6.0	7.7	0.04%	0.05%
Timber and wooden furniture industries	11.9	3.8	0.13%	0.04%
Man. of paper and paper products; printing and publishing	8.6	8.1	0.03%	0.03%
Processing of rubber and plastics	4.1	3.6	0.03%	0.03%
Other manufacturing industries	0.8	1.2	0.02%	0.04%
Construction	59.4	59.4	0.08%	0.08%
Wholesale distribution	18.8	5.9	MISSING	MISSING
Dealing in scrap and waste materials	2.5	2.5	MISSING	MISSING
Commission agents	MISSING	0.2	MISSING	MISSING
Retail distribution	45.8	15.7	MISSING	MISSING
Hotels and catering	16.5	8.1	MISSING	MISSING
Repair of consumer goods and vehicles	1.7	1.3	MISSING	MISSING
Transport and communication	12.7	6.3	MISSING	MISSING
Banking, finance, insurance, business services, leasing	25.5	4.4	MISSING	MISSING
Other services	45.0	19.6	MISSING	MISSING
All economic activities	366.0	416.3	MISSING	MISSING

LIKELY FUTURE TRENDS

E.25 In order to estimate the future impact of any increase in landfill costs on industry and commerce, employment forecasts were used for the year 2000. These showed that overall there is likely to be an increase of 2% in employment although growth and decline varies considerably between different industries. Table E.4 over the page shows the impact of a nominal £5 increase in landfill costs for the year 2000 on UK businesses. It should be noted that no forecasts of gross output are available; it has therefore been assumed that this will increase in line with employment. Table E.3 shows the changes in employment, and hence the changes in waste generation, expected to have occurred by the year 2000. It can be seen that industrial employment levels are expected to fall, especially within the primary sector, while employment within the service sector is generally expected to rise.

Table E.3: Changes in Waste Generation Expected to have Occurred by 2000

Standard Industrial Classification 1980		% change 1991 - 2000
11 - 17	Primary and utilities	-24%
21 - 49	Manufacturing	-12%
50	Construction	-3%
61, 64/65	Wholesale & Retail Distribution	+1%
62, 63, 67	Other Distribution; Repairs	-0.5%
66	Hotels and Catering	+6.5%
71 -79	Transport and Communication	-8%
81 - 85	Banking, Finance, Insurance etc	+16%
91 - 98	Other services	+8%
11 - 98	ALL SECTORS	+2%

E.26 The dramatic decline in employment, and hence waste generation, expected to occur in primary and manufacturing industry is reflected in the estimated costs of a nominal £5 increase in landfill price in the year 2000 as presented in Table E.4.

E.27 When compared to the present estimates as presented in Table E.2, the cost to SIC Class 41/42 as estimated from the survey data, for example, is expected to fall from £28 million to £24 million while the costs to Banking, Finance, Insurance, Business Services and Leasing (SIC Classes 81-85) will rise from £25 million to £30 million. Overall, the total costs to industry and commerce fall by 3% from £366 million to £355 million using the survey data and by 9% from £416 to £378 million using the Waste Disposal Plan data by the year 2000. However, the relative costs expressed as a percentage of annual gross output are the same as those presented in Table E.2 since gross output figures have also been indexed using projected changes in employment. It is likely that there is a far more complex relationship between gross output levels and employment which may lead to different relative values being produced, however.

Table E.4: Estimated Impact of a £5 Increase in Landfill Price (Year 2000)

INDUSTRY GROUP	COST OF A £5 INCREASE IN LANDFILL PRICE (£ MILLION)		COST OF INCREASE AS % OF OUTPUT	
	Survey data	WDP data	Survey data	WDP data
Coal extraction; coke ovens; extraction of oil and gas etc	3.4	9.9	0.01	0.04
Prod and dist of electricity, gas and other forms of energy	4.5	14.6	0.02	0.05
Water supply industry	0.2	3.6	0.01	0.16
Extraction and preparation of metalliferous mineral ores	MISSING	MISSING	MISSING	MISSING
Metal manufacturing	7.5	36.7	0.07	0.33
Extraction of minerals not elsewhere specified	not sig	7.6	not sig	1.23
Manufacture of non-metallic mineral products	9.2	46.7	0.09	0.47
Chemical industry	9.4	82.6	0.03	0.28
Production of man-made fibres	not sig	1.6	not sig	0.18
Manufacture of metal goods not elsewhere specified	8.4	2.7	0.07	0.02
Mechanical engineering	8.9	6.7	0.03	0.02
Manufacture of office machinery & data processing equip.	not sig	0.7	not sig	0.01
Electrical and electronic engineering	5.6	4.9	0.02	0.02
Manufacture of motor vehicles and parts thereof	6.1	2.2	0.03	0.01
Manufacture of other transport equipment	3.0	2.2	0.02	0.02
Instrument engineering	2.2	0.8	0.06	0.02
Food, drink and tobacco manufacturing industries	24.2	8.4	0.05	0.02
Textiles, leather and leather goods, footwear and clothing	5.3	6.8	0.04	0.05
Timber and wooden furniture industries	10.5	3.3	0.13	0.04
Man. of paper and paper products; printing and publishing	7.6	7.2	0.03	0.03
Processing of rubber and plastics	3.6	3.2	0.03	0.03
Other manufacturing industries	0.7	1.1	0.02	0.04
Construction	57.6	57.6	0.08	0.08
Wholesale distribution	18.9	6.0	MISSING	MISSING
Dealing in scrap and waste materials	2.5	2.5	MISSING	MISSING
Commission agents	MISSING	0.2	MISSING	MISSING
Retail distribution	46.3	15.8	MISSING	MISSING
Hotels and catering	17.6	8.6	MISSING	MISSING
Repair of consumer goods and vehicles	1.7	1.3	MISSING	MISSING
Transport and communication	11.7	5.8	MISSING	MISSING
Banking, finance, insurance, business services, leasing	29.6	5.1	MISSING	MISSING
Other services	48.6	21.2	MISSING	MISSING
All economic activities	354.8	377.6	MISSING	MISSING

9

ESTIMATING WASTE COMPOSITION

E.28 Information on the composition of waste is relevant to the project as landfill price generally increases proportional to the difficulty of the waste in terms of its reactivity. Special waste, for example, attracts a far higher charge than inert waste. There are two principal sources of information available on the composition of waste being disposed of to landfill. These are Waste Disposal Plans and raw survey data.

E.29 Both sets were initially examined for suitability and it was concluded that the distribution of the composition of waste varied dramatically from county to county. For this reason, it was decided not to use the raw survey data from which suitable data were available for only one county but rather to use the Waste Disposal Plan data. The results are presented in Table E.5. The range reflects the high and low proportions of the total waste attributable to each category across the counties providing data. For example, in one county none of the waste being landfilled was inorganic acids whereas in another inorganic acids accounted for 2% of the total. The median value was taken to represent the average percentage of total waste going to landfill in the UK attributable to each category. This figure was then multiplied by the estimates of total waste going to landfill derived from each of the two sources of data (survey data and Waste Disposal Plans).

Table E.5: Estimated composition of waste being landfilled in the UK

DoE Waste Category	Range (%)	Median (%)	Quantity landfilled (survey data) ('000 tonnes)	Quantity landfilled (WDP data) ('000 tonnes)
A - Inorganic Acids	0 - 2	<1	not sig	not sig
B - Organic Acids	0	<1	not sig	not sig
C - Alkalis	0 - 2	<1	not sig	not sig
D - Toxic Metal Compounds	0 - 4	1	732	833
E - Non- Toxic Metal Compounds	0 - 1	<1	not sig	not sig
F - Metals (Elemental)	0 - 19	1	732	833
G - Metal Oxides	0	<1	not sig	not sig
H - Inorganic Compounds	0 - 1	<1	not sig	not sig
J - Other Inorganic Compounds	17 - 59	44	32,215	36,637
K - Organic Compounds	0	<1	not sig	not sig
L - Polymeric Materials	1 - 3	1	732	833
M - Fuels, Oils and Greases	0 - 4	2	1,464	1,665
N - Fine Chemicals etc	0	<1	not sig	not sig
P - Miscellaneous Chemical Waste	0 - 1	<1	not sig	not sig
Q - Filter Materials etc	0 - 27	2	1,464	1,665
R - Interceptor Wastes	1 - 4	2	1,464	1,665
S - Miscellaneous Waste	6 - 48	38	27,822	31,640
T - Animal and Food Waste	3 - 48	9	6,589	7,494
U - Clinical Waste	0 - 6	<1	not sig	not sig
		100%	73,214	83,265

E.30 Most of the waste falls within categories J (Other Inorganic Compounds) and S (Miscellaneous Waste). These will cover materials such as metal, paper, cardboard and inert and non-inert construction waste. There is clearly need for further research if information is required in any more detail than that provided here.

ESTIMATING THE PRESENT COSTS OF LANDFILL

E.31 Information on the cost to businesses of waste landfilling is relevant to the project as it provides a measure of the relative impact of an increase in the price of landfill. For example, a £5 per tonne increase on waste that costs £50 per tonne to landfill would not be particularly significant whereas £5 per tonne on waste that only costs £1 per tonne would represent a dramatic increase.

E.32 Costs vary considerably according to market conditions and geographical location of the site. Various estimates have been published in recent years, however, and are summarised below:

Howard Humphreys estimate for construction and demolition wastes (excluding transport costs)	£1 - £3 per tonne (inert) £3 - £16 per tonne (contaminated)
British Scrap Federation estimate (excluding transport costs)	£11 per tonne (average)
Estimate derived from an **Aspinwall and Company** estimate	£6.50 - £13 per tonne
Coopers and Lybrand estimate for household and commercial waste	£5 - £30 per tonne
KPMG Management Consulting estimate for 1990 annual turnover from landfill of £950 million divided by best estimate of amount of waste landfilled	About £10 per tonne (average for all controlled waste)

E.33 It can therefore be concluded that although accurate figures on the costs of landfill to businesses are not available, these are likely to fall within the range of £1 to £30 per tonne (except for certain special wastes) with an overall average of around £10 per tonne. Costs are partly dependant on the type of material being landfilled and partly dependant on the area of the country within which the landfill site is situated. Further research would be needed if more refined estimates were to be required and similarly if costs to each sector of industry were needed.

PRIORITIES FOR FURTHER RESEARCH

E.34 The estimates provided in this report are the best available. However, there are clear priorities for further research in several areas, some of which is already planned or being undertaken. The areas can be summarised as follows.

1. **Waste Arisings Surveys**
    Research into the best methods for conducting surveys of industrial and commercial waste producers including:

    -   best practice sampling procedures. A good deal of expertise in this area already exists within Waste Regulation Authorities and in other European member states.

    -   research into the most appropriate volume to weight conversion factors to be used for converting volumetric survey results.

2. **Sources of General Industrial and Commercial Waste**
    Research on the types of sources of general industrial and commercial waste (GIW) within the producer's premises. This approach would be based on a waste auditing methodology, identifying the various processes, sources and pathways of waste within the producer's premises. From this, a predictive modelling exercise could be conducted to identify the most appropriate proxy variables (floorspace, production capacity, gross output, energy consumption or number of employees, for example) for different industry sectors.

3. **Estimation and Forecasting of Arisings**
    Further progress in estimating and forecasting requires that progress is made on understanding sources and pathways of waste within the producer's premises, as outlined above. Once this has been achieved, estimation and forecasting methods can be further developed and improved. Forecasting, in particular, should be based on projections of structural and technological change (such as process changes and product substitution) as well as baseline forecasts in the proxy variable.

4. **Waste Disposal Surveys**
    Further research into the quantity of waste being landfilled. Information may be available through the site licensing returns received by the Waste Regulation Authorities although some attempt to tie these figures to the industry of origin would ideally be required.

5. **Costs of Waste Disposal to Industry**
    Research into the costs of disposal for the various different waste disposal methods and the costs borne by each sector of industry.

6.   **Waste Composition**

Research into the composition of waste both being generated and being landfilled including, for example, the amount of packaging waste and recyclable industrial and commercial waste being landfilled.

1 BACKGROUND AND INTRODUCTION

Terms of Reference

1.1 The key terms of reference for this study were to:

1. Review sources of information on the industrial breakdown, composition and price of disposal of industrial and commercial waste arising and going to landfill in the UK.

2. Provide best estimates, for the most recent year and likely future trends, of the tonnes per year of such waste arising and going to landfill, by main SIC group and where possible for key groups.

1.2 Appendix 1 of this report sets out in some detail the methods used to derive estimates of waste arising and going to landfill in the UK by industry sector of origin. We believes that it is more informative to the reader to detail all potential sources of error rather than to lead readers to believe that the figures presented accurately reflect reality. We are confident, however, that the figures presented are the best available and the detailed breakdown of assumptions and errors should be taken as demonstrating our technical rigour rather than as an expression of a lack of confidence in the results. Overall, therefore, we have sought to achieve two goals: firstly to present the estimated quantities of industrial and commercial waste going to landfill in the UK together with the consequential impact of any increase in landfill price; and secondly, and equally importantly, to describe the limitations of the current data and to point to ways in which the quality could be improved in the future.

Structure of the Report

1.3 This report is divided into ten chapters. This chapter, the background and introduction, places the study in its policy context, states the aims and objectives of the project, lists the scope of the study together with the definitions used throughout and reviews the knowledge base of statistics on industrial and commercial waste in the UK. Chapter 2 provides a brief overview of the methods adopted for this study while Chapters 3 and 4 provide a description of the methods used for each stage of the calculation. Chapter 5 details the refinements that have been made to the data while Chapter 6 provides estimates of the impact on industry of any increase in landfill price. Chapter 7 provides a prediction of likely future trends, Chapter 8 gives details of the composition of the waste going to landfill and Chapter 9 provides an indication of the present costs of landfill.

Aims and Objectives

1.4 The aim of the study is to provide the Department of the Environment with a statistical basis upon which to estimate the likely increase in waste disposal costs to each sector of industry and commerce should policies be introduced which affect the price of landfill in the UK.

1.5 As information on controlled industrial and commercial waste going to landfill is not currently available in this format, the objectives of the study can be described as follows:

1. Produce estimates of controlled industrial and commercial waste arising in the UK by industry of origin.

2. Produce estimates of the proportion of this being landfilled in the UK by industry of origin.

3. Provide estimates of the costs of a £5 per tonne increase in the price of landfill to each sector of industry and commerce, in terms of the total estimated costs and as a percentage of gross output.

4. Provide an indication of the composition of this waste.

5. Provide an indication of likely future trends in waste generation and hence the future cost to businesses of any increase in landfill price

Scope and Definitions

1.6 **Controlled industrial and commercial waste** has been defined as industrial waste (including construction and demolition waste) and commercial waste (including that collected by the public sector or their contractors).

1.7 **Industry of origin** is defined by the Standard Industrial Classification (SIC)[1]. Various versions of this nomenclature are available, the first of which was produced in 1968, updated in 1980, and the latest being published in 1992 in order to make the UK's system compatible with the European standard (NACE). For the purposes of this project, the 1980 version of SIC has been used throughout, converting from the 1968 version where necessary. This decision was taken so that data obtained are compatible with economic data such as the Census of Employment[2] and the Census of Production[3] and with the information published in the Waste Disposal Plans of the Waste Disposal and Regulation Authorities. The timing of the project made the use of the 1992 SIC impractical as no official conversion from 1980 SIC is yet available although this should not preclude such a conversion being undertaken in the future on the data included in this report. It should also be noted that the Standard Industrial Classification is applied to each unit of production or premises.

1.8 **Waste composition** is defined according to the Department of the Environment classification as published in the draft Waste Management Paper 2/3. Although information was required in less detail (inert and non-inert), it was not possible to adequately transpose data included in the Waste Disposal Plans in DoE coding format into these two broader categories.

1.9 **Waste landfilled** excludes that being recycled, reused, incinerated, composted, disposed of to the water course or otherwise treated.

1.10 **Price for landfill** has been taken to mean the total cost to businesses of their waste disposal per tonne of waste taken to landfill (including transport costs) rather than simply the price for disposal at the landfill gate.

Policy Context of the Research

1.11 The Government has indicated its intention in the Environment White Paper and Sustainable Development UK Strategy to use market-based instruments as well as regulation and traditional methods of control to support its policies on the environment. One such economic instrument is a proposed levy on the landfilling of waste.

1.12 Three main pieces of research have been commissioned by the Government to examine the effect of applying economic instruments to the disposal of waste. The results of the research have been published as:

Economic Instruments and Recovery of Resources from Waste
(ERL: HMSO 1992)[4]

Landfill Costs and Prices: Correcting Possible Market Distortions
(Coopers and Lybrand: HMSO 1993)[5]

Externalities from Landfill and Incineration
(CSERGE, Warren Spring Laboratory and EFTEL: HMSO 1993)[6]

1.13 The ERL report introduces the general application of economic instruments for environmental protection, the Coopers and Lybrand report focuses principally on household and commercial waste and the Externalities report concentrates on the externalities of disposing of the entire controlled waste stream. None of the reports provides an estimate of the distribution of costs that would be incurred by industry and commerce as a whole as a result of waste disposal firms passing on the cost of a levy to their customers. This information will assist in assessing the likely costs to business of present policy proposals, such as that for a landfill tax, as well as informing the direction of future waste disposal policy.

The State of Statistics on Industrial and Commercial Waste in the UK

1.14 It has long been acknowledged that there is a need for more reliable information on the quantities and composition of industrial and commercial waste in the UK. For example, the eleventh report of the Royal Commission on Environmental Pollution (Managing Waste: The Duty of Care)[7], published in 1985, stated:

> *We have concluded that there is insufficient reliable information available about industrial waste generation. Without this information we do not consider that waste disposal authorities can properly prepare waste disposal plans for their areas ..... we recommend that the Government should consider ways of improving the quality and comprehensiveness of published statistics on controlled industrial wastes.*
> p 27

Waste Arisings

1.15 Most of the difficulties with estimating quantities of industrial and commercial waste are methodological and technical.

1.16 For example, in many areas it is impossible to carry out a 100% survey of firms due to the large numbers involved and the consequent implications on staff time and resources. The only practical alternative is to carry out a sample survey of the smaller firms. However, there must then be a method for estimating the quantity of waste arising from those firms not surveyed, as represented by the sample. Waste Management Papers 2 and 3[8,9] recommend that employment is used as an indicator (tonnes of waste per employee per annum) although there is a long standing controversy over this method. M.E.L Research has carried out research into the relationship between waste generation and employment and has concluded that for many sectors of industry and commerce there is not a linear relationship between the quantity of waste generated at a particular premises and the number of people employed there. Whatever indicator is used, be it employment, gross output, turnover, floorspace, energy usage or others, there must be information available on it for both the firm being surveyed and for the area for which survey estimates are to be made. Research conducted principally by M.E.L Research and Aspinwall and Company[10] as part of the first stage of the General Industrial Waste project has shown that such data are often difficult to acquire. The only readily available source would appear to be the Census of Employment and even this is restricted to planning uses only. It is also interesting to note that research in Europe, notably in Germany, has concluded that employment is the most practical and accurate estimator available. It is our belief that in the absence of suitable alternative national data, employment (tonnes per employee per annum) should be used as an estimator for waste generation, although the errors intrinsic in this approach should be always borne in mind.

1.17 Although the current state of data on industrial and commercial waste is not satisfactory, a project jointly funded by the Department of the Environment and the Department of Trade and Industry known as the General Industrial Waste project (GIW), is seeking to generate a predictive model for such wastes that will hopefully overcome the need to rely exclusively on employment data. It is currently at an exploratory stage, however, and final results are not expected for several years.

Waste Disposal to Landfill

1.18 Data on industrial waste being disposed of are available from the companies operating disposal sites, although this information is regarded as commercially sensitive and therefore extremely difficult to obtain except where its provision is a statutory requirement. Such a requirement is made in the licences issued by the Waste Regulation Authorities; each disposal site must make a return to their authority stating the quantity of each type of waste they have accepted in the period since the last return. Returns for inert sites are generally made annually while for sites licensed to accept household waste and hazardous waste, returns are often required more frequently. Although data are available from this source, information is rarely aggregated and in many cases is supplied in a non-standard format; in addition, doubts have been expressed about its accuracy and one particular issue is the fact that waste is often not weighed. These data are rarely published in the Waste Disposal Plans as authorities are required to survey arisings and not deposits of waste. In any case, the data obtained in this way will not relate the quantity deposited to the industry of origin, a prerequisite for the task in hand.

Waste Composition

1.19 The composition of waste can be determined either from a survey at the premises where it is produced or at the disposal site from site returns. There are interpretative problems with each source, however. Information from companies can either be based on a personal visit where the inspector estimates the composition of each waste container, generally only noting down the principal component. Alternatively, a postal survey approach leaves the estimation to the producer. There are bound to be respondent errors in either approach. The use of site returns is equally problematic as returns are made on the basis of categories of waste specified in the site licence. These can be as vague as 'industrial waste' or as detailed as the Waste Disposal Authority feels is justified; licences for hazardous waste sites, for example, are more specific. Combining data from different Waste Disposal Authorities from this source will therefore be extremely difficult and will almost certainly result in the use of the lowest common denominator such that information is practically useless for determining composition.

1.20 In summary, statistics on industrial and commercial waste have not become any more accurate since the Royal Commission's 11th report of 1985; published data are therefore likely to contain errors which can not be corrected. It is therefore necessary to reiterate that figures published here are *best available estimates* of waste arising and disposed of to landfill in the UK.

2 OVERVIEW OF METHODS

Introduction

2.1 There is no information directly available on the quantities and types of industrial and commercial waste being landfilled in the UK according to industry of origin. However, there is information that can be used to estimate the quantity and composition of waste arising within each sector of industry and commerce and there is also limited information on the quantity and type of waste being landfilled although not by industry of origin. There are therefore two options open for estimating the quantity and type of waste being landfilled:

1. Use the data on waste arisings by industry sector and apply a factor to each to estimate the proportion being landfilled

2. Use the data on waste disposals and try to work backwards to determine the likely industries of origin.

2.2 As in this project it is the industry of origin that is most important for assessing the likely costs to be incurred if a policy instrument based on tonnages of waste being landfilled were to be introduced, it was decided that the former method would be used, cross-referring to the second set of data in order to be confident that estimates are of the correct order of magnitude. This method is likely to produce the most accurate estimation of the relative distribution of waste being landfilled across the various sectors of industry and commerce.

Estimating Waste Arisings

2.3 There are three main sources of data on waste arising in the UK:

1. Data published in Waste Disposal Plans
2. Raw survey data from Waste Regulation Authorities
3. Other published survey results

2.4 As stated earlier in the report, the estimation of waste arisings is based on employment data (tonnes per employee per annum). This kind of estimation procedure is needed because the data available do not cover the whole of the United Kingdom; waste for the missing areas must therefore be estimated from the results of the surveyed areas.

Waste Disposal Plans

2.5 The data that have been collected have come from surveys carried out by Waste Disposal and Regulation Authorities under their duty to produce a Waste Disposal Plan. This requirement was first implemented under the Control of Pollution Act 1974 and reinforced under Section 50 of the Environmental Protection Act 1990. Guidance for undertaking the survey is given to Waste Disposal and Regulation Authorities in Waste Management Paper 2: Waste Disposal Surveys, first published in 1976 with an update currently being circulated in draft by the Department of the Environment. The 1976 Waste Management Paper, under whose guidance all the Waste Disposal Plans were produced, recommends:

> *As most authorities do not have access to data on the volume of waste produced by firms in their area it is necessary to find a measure readily available to authorities which will reflect the amount of waste being produced. Two substitute or proxy variables which suggest themselves are the number of persons employed and the rateable values. While it is generally felt that the number of persons employed is a better measure of waste produced, in some cases this will not be available and rateable value will have to be used.*
>
> *p 6*

2.6 The Waste Management Paper goes on to explain how to estimate total waste arising from a sample:

> *Estimates of waste for the whole group can be made by assuming that the waste per man within the group is equal to the waste per man calculated from the sample.*
>
> *p 7*

2.7 The data that are included within the Waste Disposal Plans have therefore already made this assumption and any errors associated with this approach are intrinsic to the data. If one was to reject this approach altogether, as has been suggested by various bodies in recent years, there would be a serious lack of data; it is our belief that any information, albeit of dubious accuracy, is better than making policy completely in the dark. While it is clear that this issue needs further investigation, a task which will be carried out under the auspices of the GIW programme, the estimation process detailed here must work within the accepted assumptions.

2.8 Data from the Waste Disposal Plans has therefore been entered onto a database and extrapolations have been made for the areas of the UK for which there are no data from this source. These extrapolations are based on waste per employee per annum coefficients, grossed up using data from the Census of Employment 1991. Further detail on this method, together with its intrinsic errors, is given in Appendix 1 of this report.

Raw Survey Data from Waste Regulation Authorities

2.9 In addition to the above source of information on waste arisings, M.E.L Research holds the raw data from a number of English Waste Regulation Authorities' waste disposal surveys. This source of data has several advantages over the published Waste Disposal Plan data, summarised below:

1. Data are provided at company level so any aggregation is possible; disaggregating published Waste Disposal Plan data is far more problematic.

2. Information on the more detailed Standard Industrial Classification *Class* (2-digit) is given; Waste Disposal Plans (with the exception of Avon's plan) aggregate data to *Division* (1-digit) level.

3. The data are all relatively recent, some as recent as 1993; the data contained in Waste Disposal Plans date from the late 70s in some cases.

4. Because the data are in a raw format, it is possible to minimise errors associated with estimating from the mean and also obtain some measure of the errors associated with the estimate.

2.10 However, this source also has disadvantages, the principal one being that the area covered by the surveys incorporates only three English counties and one metropolitan district (West Midlands, Humberside, Norfolk and Sheffield), totalling 2% of all UK employment. Grossing up on the basis of tonnes of waste per employee per annum derived from these surveys for areas as diverse as the Scottish Islands and central London may bias the results. The limited amount of statistical testing we have been able to perform on the data would suggest, however, that for the majority of industry sectors there are no significant geographical differences between tonnes per employee coefficients.

Other Published Survey Results

2.11 In addition to the Waste Disposal Plans and the raw survey data, there are two additional surveys for which results have been published. The first is a study conducted in 1978 by A R Tron[11] at Warren Spring Laboratory with the aim of estimating the potential for recovery of industrial and commercial wastes arising in Britain; the second is an unpublished Warren Spring Laboratory study[12] carried out in 1983 which also provides estimates of industrial and commercial waste generated by each industry sector. Details of both these studies have been obtained from a review report produced by Aspinwall and Company[13].

2.12 In view of the fact that all the sources mentioned above are prone to various statistical errors, the results of each will be compared at the end of Chapter 3. From this comparison it may be possible to decide which sets of data are most appropriate for estimating the quantities of waste sent for landfill in the UK by each sector of industry.

Estimating Waste Disposals

2.13 Very little information is directly available on the use of waste disposal routes by the industry of origin. The main secondary source for this data has been the *Externalities from Landfill and Incineration* report.

Information on Annual Gross Output

2.14 Information on the aggregated annual gross output of companies in the UK was obtained from the Census of Production, data relating to 1991. Unfortunately this Census only covers manufacturing industry and no comparable source of information could be found for commerce and construction. Information on the cost to each sector of industry as a percentage of the annual gross output of that sector can then be calculated in order to determine which sectors would be particularly affected by an increase in the costs of disposal to landfill.

3 CALCULATION OF TOTAL INDUSTRIAL AND COMMERCIAL WASTE ARISING

Introduction

3.1 Waste arising refers to all waste being produced by, in this case, industry and commerce (including the construction industry). This includes waste recycled, although not waste reused internally by companies. It specifically excludes waste arising from agriculture, forestry and fishing activities (Division 0) as these are not currently classified as controlled wastes and, as a result, the data available on quantities are unreliable. In any case, it is likely that only a very small proportion of agricultural waste is disposed of to licensed landfill sites.

3.2 This chapter provides an overview of how these estimates have been derived from available data on industrial and commercial waste arising in the UK. Further detail on the methodology is included as Appendix 1. Two key sources of data were used to separately produce estimates, slightly different estimation methods being used for each source. These are:

1. Waste Disposal Plans
2. Raw data from surveys carried out by M.E.L Research and Waste Disposal and Regulation Authorities

3.3 Estimates produced using the two sources of data are presented at the end of the chapter in Table 3.1.

3.4 In addition, estimates produced from other published sources and data obtained from other European member states have been included for comparative purposes as Appendix 2 and Appendix 4.

Background to the Data Used in the Project

Methodology

3.5 Data from all of the sources above were produced using the same basic methodology. The most commonly used approach to calculating waste arisings is a survey of a producer's premises. This study uses the data obtained through surveys carried out by Waste Disposal and Regulation Authorities in England who have generally followed the methodology suggested in Waste Management Paper 2. In summary, this involves a census of companies employing more than 1000 staff and a sample survey of the remainder.

Methodology Used in this Project

3.6   The object of this part of the study was to derive an estimate for total industrial and commercial waste arising in the UK. Each source of secondary data was therefore examined for useful data, the most important factor being that a breakdown of waste arising within each sector of industry be available.

Data from the Waste Disposal Plans

3.7   Each Waste Disposal Plan was systematically reviewed and relevant data were extracted.

3.8   The estimation process consisted of five stages, as follows:

1.   Conversion of data in 1968 Standard Industrial Classification format to 1980 Standard Industrial Classification Divisions
2.   Filling in the gaps for counties and districts with no data to produce regional and national estimates
3.   Estimation for areas not covered by the Waste Disposal Plans (Scotland, Wales and Northern Ireland)
4.   Disaggregation from SIC Division to SIC Class
5.   Production of total quantities by grouped SIC Classes for the UK

3.9   Each stage of the estimation process listed above is described in detail in Appendix 1.

Raw Data from Surveys

3.10 M.E.L Research holds the raw data from three counties' Waste Disposal Plan surveys (West Midlands, Humberside and Norfolk) and data from a survey of commercial firms in Sheffield, carried out on behalf of a consortium comprising the DoE, DTi, FoE and INCPEN. In total, this equates to a database holding information on 2918 firms in the UK representing 2% of all UK employment. As the data are in a raw format, the sources of error can be controlled far more tightly than is possible when using secondary data, such as that contained in the Waste Disposal Plans. Although the data only relate to three counties and one district in England, it is possible to have much greater confidence in the basic data than those from the Waste Disposal Plans described above.

3.11 The calculation process involved three stages, as follows:

1.   Conversion of data into a compatible format and derivation of a tonnes per employee figure for each firm
2.   Production of an average tonnes per employee figure for each SIC Class
3.   Estimation for the UK

3.12 This is described in detail in Appendix 1.

Published results of independent surveys

3.13 The results of two independent surveys are cited in a report by Aspinwall and Company[13] on the techniques used to determine industrial and commercial waste arisings. They are included as an illustration of the different estimates of tonnes per employee that may be derived from different surveys. As the resulting estimates are so different to other published figures and those derived from the Waste Disposal Plans and survey data, they are included in Appendix 4 for illustrative purposes only.

Data Carried Forward

3.14 As Table 3.1 over the page shows, the estimate of total waste arising in the UK derived from the Waste Disposal Plan data is around 121 million tonnes while the estimate derived from the survey data is slightly lower at 85 million tonnes. Both sets will be carried forward to estimate the impact on industry of an increase in landfill price and will be refined in Chapter 5 of the report. Some discussion on the differences between the two data sets is also included in this chapter.

Table 3.1: Comparison of Industrial and Commercial Waste Arisings Estimates Derived from the Two Sources of Data to be Carried Forward

INDUSTRY GROUP	TONNES OF WASTE ARISING PER ANNUM		DIFFERENCE BETWEEN THE TWO DATA SETS (TONNES)
	Survey data	WDP data	
Coal extraction; coke ovens; extraction of oil and gas etc	1,227,366	3,561,666	-2,334,330
Prod and dist of electricity, gas and other forms of energy	1,628,647	5,249,218	-3,620,571
Water supply industry	82,585	1,299,403	-1,216,818
Extraction and preparation of metalliferous mineral ores	MISSING	MISSING	MISSING
Metal manufacturing	2,329,630	11,416,662	-9,087,032
Extraction of minerals not elsewhere specified	7,203	2,356,402	-2,349,199
Manufacture of non-metallic mineral products	2,878,755	14,535,453	-11,656,698
Chemical industry	2,939,826	25,713,555	-22,774,729
Production of man-made fibres	12,337	497,138	-484,801
Manufacture of metal goods not elsewhere specified	2,616,247	852,107	1,764,140
Mechanical engineering	2,775,275	2,078,661	696,614
Manufacture of office machinery & data processing equip.	10,485	219,798	-209,313
Electrical and electronic engineering	1,758,883	1,531,461	227,422
Manufacture of motor vehicles and parts thereof	1,896,946	690,729	1,206,217
Manufacture of other transport equipment	933,025	686,275	246,750
Instrument engineering	669,868	259,494	410,374
Food, drink and tobacco manufacturing industries	7,549,395	2,606,805	4,942,590
Textiles, leather and leather goods, footwear and clothing	1,635,709	2,103,370	-467,661
Timber and wooden furniture industries	3,262,746	1,028,706	2,234,040
Man. of paper and paper products; printing and publishing	2,367,644	2,230,929	136,714
Processing of rubber and plastics	1,116,208	995,996	120,212
Other manufacturing industries	207,439	338,361	-130,922
Construction	4,581,540	25,809,673	-21,228,133
Wholesale distribution	4,689,792	1,485,526	3,204,266
Dealing in scrap and waste materials	1,974,276	30,877	1,943,399
Commission agents	MISSING	55,552	MISSING
Retail distribution	11,454,148	3,916,666	7,537,482
Hotels and catering	4,114,371	2,017,035	2,097,336
Repair of consumer goods and vehicles	415,522	323,408	92,114
Transport and communication	3,184,630	1,568,512	1,616,118
Banking, finance, insurance, business services, leasing	6,370,334	1,109,048	5,261,285
Other services	11,240,522	4,912,443	6,328,079
All economic activities	**85,930,320**	**121,480,928**	**-35,550,608**

26

4 CALCULATING WASTE BEING LANDFILLED

Introduction

4.1 The previous chapter has described how estimates were made for industrial and commercial waste arising in the UK. This chapter describes how estimates of waste being landfilled were derived from the arisings estimates included in Table 3.1.

4.2 There is very little information on the disposal routes for industrial, commercial waste and construction waste. There are no data on the proportion of waste going to landfill sites by the industry of origin. It is difficult to know how to obtain this data even given an unlimited timescale and budget for data collection. With the introduction of the Duty of Care in 1992, producers are now more likely to know the destination of their waste so one possibility would be for Waste Regulation Authorities to determine this in the surveys they must carry out for the Waste Disposal Plans required under Section 50 of the Environmental Protection Act. Another possibility would be to collect this data from the site records of disposal firms. In either case, this data collection exercise is beyond the remit of this project.

Sources of Data

4.3 One main source of information on the proportion of waste going to landfill was used. This is the Externalities report produced for the Department of the Environment by CSERGE *et al.* Estimates included in this report were derived from published figures and discussions with the Department of the Environment. It should be noted that the figure for construction and demolition waste quoted differs from the most recently published figure of 70 million tonnes. This is partly because the research from which it is derived was not available to the authors of the Externalities report, but also because the higher figure includes inert arisings such as excavated soil and clay; materials such as concrete, masonry and steel arisings from the construction and demolition of man-made structures accounts for approximately 24 million tonnes. In addition, much of the waste may be put to a useful purpose at the landfill site.

4.4 In the Executive Summary of the Externalities report, two tables are included (E.1 and E.2) giving tonnages of broad types of waste going to landfill and to incineration. These have been combined and the totals reproduced below. .

Table 4.1: Summary of Controlled Waste and Percentage Landfilled

Waste Type	Total Arising	Total Landfilled	Total Incinerated	Total Other Disposal	% of Total Landfilled
Household inc. Civic Amenity	20	16.9	2.2	0.9	**84.5**
Commercial	15	14.3	0.8	0.0	**95.0**
Construction and Demolition	32	14.8	0.0	17.2	**46.0**
Industrial	64	47.0	0.0	17.0	**73.0**
All other waste	14	9.0	0.9	4.1	**64.0**

source: Externalities From Landfill and Incineration (CSERGE, WSL, EFTEL)

4.5 This source would therefore suggest that 46% of construction waste is landfilled, 73% of industrial waste is landfilled and that 95% of commercial waste is landfilled. This latter estimate is somewhat suspect, however, as it is suggested that no, or very little, commercial waste is recycled or reused. However, M.E.L Research has conducted several surveys of commercial waste producers which would suggest that between 8% and 30% of this type of waste is recycled[14,15].

Data Used in this Project

4.6 The data used for this study are therefore based primarily on the data published in the Externalities from Landfill and Incineration report. The figure for commercial waste going to landfill has been refined based on M.E.L Research's knowledge of commercial waste recycling, however. The data used are therefore:

Industrial waste 73% landfilled
Construction waste 46% landfilled
Commercial waste 80% landfilled

4.7 As mentioned above, there are no available data relating to the disposal routes for waste by the industry of origin. It has therefore had to be assumed that each industry sector within the broad headings listed above landfills the same proportion of waste. This is unlikely to be the case in reality, particularly in the light of the drive towards reducing the risk of potential environmental legacies that has taken place within various industries over the last few years. This is an area that would need further research if more precise data were to be required. This is beyond the remit of this project, however, as the brief was to utilise all *available* data.

5 REFINEMENTS TO THE DATA SETS

Refining the Estimates

5.1 Having produced the estimates of quantities of industrial and commercial waste going to landfill in the UK, some of the figures needed refining in the light of comments received by trade organisations and other sources of information. In particular, more accurate data exists for the construction industry (SIC Class 50) and for dealers in scrap and waste materials (SIC Class 62). Table 5.1 shows the effects of the refinements.

Waste from the Construction Industry

5.2 The quantity of construction waste arising and going to landfill is particularly difficult to estimate due to variability over time and the fact that much of this type of waste is reused at source. In addition, waste entering a landfill site is often not considered to be waste since some will be used for road hardening. A report to the Department of the Environment by Howard Humphreys entitled *Managing Demolition and Construction Waste* (HMSO 1994) has estimated the quantity of construction and demolition waste being landfilled in the UK and is regarded as the most accurate source of data on this type of waste. Howard Humphreys estimate that a total of 42 million tonnes of waste from the construction industry is disposed of at landfill sites annually in the UK. Some of this, however, is put to a useful purpose on site and as such is not actually landfilled. The total quantity of construction waste being **landfilled** is therefore estimated to be around 30 million tonnes. This is higher than the figure cited in the recently published government publication - *Sustainable Development: The UK Strategy* of 17 million tonnes, greater than the estimate derived from the Waste Disposal Plan data of 11 million tonnes and considerably greater than that derived from the survey data of 2 million tonnes. In the absence of comments on the Howard Humphreys report and after much consideration, it was decided to standardise on the Waste Disposal Plan estimate rather than the Howard Humphreys estimate since it corresponds more closely to existing sources of data.

Waste from Dealers in Scrap and Waste Materials

5.3 This sector of industry is problematic in that it refers to companies dealing in scrap and waste as well as producing their own waste. The two sets of data on this sector are very different, the Waste Disposal Plans suggesting it generates nearly 2 million tonnes per annum while the survey data suggests that this is just over 30,000 tonnes. The probable explanation for this is that some surveys will have included the waste or scrap that the companies are dealing in as their waste while others will have quantified only the waste produced by their own offices. The former method will count some waste twice in an overall waste balance. This project is intended to assess the impact of an increase in the costs of landfill to industry as a whole and it assumes that the full cost of the levy will be passed on to the waste disposal contractor's customers. It would therefore count the costs twice if the higher figure was to be used. The British Scrap Federation supplied information that of the 9 million tonnes of scrap their members collect each year, around 400,000 tonnes is "liberated to landfill" at a cost of around £11 per tonne. The true figure is therefore likely to lie somewhere between these points and is not possible to determine with any accuracy. For producing estimates, a nominal figure of 500,000 tonnes has been used.

Table 5.1: Refined Estimates of Waste Arising and Waste Going to Landfill in the UK each Year

INDUSTRY GROUP	TONNES OF WASTE ARISING PER ANNUM		TONNES OF WASTE LANDFILLED PER ANNUM	
	Survey data	WDP data	Survey data	WDP data
Coal extraction; coke ovens; extraction of oil and gas etc	1,227,336	3,561,666	895,955	2,600,017
Prod and dist of electricity, gas and other forms of energy	1,628,647	5,249,218	1,188,912	3,831,929
Water supply industry	82,585	1,299,403	60,287	948,564
Extraction and preparation of metalliferous mineral ores	MISSING	MISSING	MISSING	MISSING
Metal manufacturing	2,329,630	11,416,662	1,700,630	8,334,163
Extraction of minerals not elsewhere specified	7,203	2,356,402	5,258	1,720,173
Manufacture of non-metallic mineral products	2,878,755	14,535,453	2,101,491	10,610,881
Chemical industry	2,938,826	25,713,555	2,145,343	18,770,895
Production of man-made fibres	12,337	497,138	9,006	362,911
Manufacture of metal goods not elsewhere specified	2,616,247	852,107	1,909,860	622,038
Mechanical engineering	2,775,275	2,078,661	2,025,951	1,517,422
Manufacture of office machinery & data processing equip.	10,485	219,798	7,654	160,453
Electrical and electronic engineering	1,758,883	1,531,461	1,283,985	1,117,967
Manufacture of motor vehicles and parts thereof	1,896,946	690,729	1,384,770	504,232
Manufacture of other transport equipment	933,025	686,275	681,108	500,981
Instrument engineering	669,868	259,494	489,004	189,431
Food, drink and tobacco manufacturing industries	7,549,395	2,606,805	5,511,058	1,902,968
Textiles, leather and leather goods, footwear and clothing	1,635,709	2,103,370	1,194,067	1,535,460
Timber and wooden furniture industries	3,262,746	1,028,706	2,381,805	750,956
Man. of paper and paper products; printing and publishing	2,367,644	2,230,929	1,728,380	1,628,578
Processing of rubber and plastics	1,116,208	995,996	814,832	727,077
Other manufacturing industries	207,439	338,361	151,430	247,003
Construction	25,809,673	25,809,673	11,872,449	11,872,449
Wholesale distribution	4,689,792	1,485,526	3,751,8363	1,118,421
Dealing in scrap and waste materials	INACCURATE	INACCURATE	500,000	500,000
Commission agents	MISSING	55,552	MISSING	44,442
Retail distribution	11,454,148	3,916,666	9,163,318	3,133,333
Hotels and catering	4,114,371	2,017,035	3,291,497	1,613,628
Repair of consumer goods and vehicles	415,522	323,408	332,417	258,726
Transport and communication	3,184,630	1,568,512	2,547,704	1,254,810
Banking, finance, insurance, business services, leasing	6,370,334	1,109,048	5,096,267	887,239
Other services	11,240,522	4,912,443	8,992,418	3,929,955
All economic activities	**105,184,181**	**121,450,052**	**73,218,689**	**83,267,102**

Discussion

5.4 Table 5.1 presents the figures that will be used to estimate the impact of an increase in landfill price on the various sectors of industry. An estimate of around 73 million tonnes is produced from the survey data while the Waste Disposal Plan data produce an estimate of 83 million tonnes of industrial and commercial waste going to landfill each year in the UK. A discussion of these observed differences is presented below.

5.5 Figure 5.1 below illustrates the industrial arisings estimates produced using the two methods. In some of the manufacturing industries, the estimates based on waste disposal plan data are much larger than the corresponding estimates based on the survey data. This is particularly true in SIC Division 2, the extraction of minerals and ores other than fuels, the manufacture of metals, mineral products and chemicals, where the estimates produced are over three times as large. The converse is true for the service industries where the estimates based on the survey data sets are significantly higher than those estimated from the disposal plans.

Figure 5.1: Graphical Comparison of the Two Data Sets

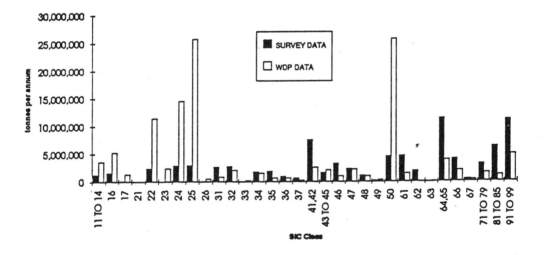

5.6 In Chapter 2 of this report, the strengths and weaknesses of the two data sources are discussed briefly. The statistical aspects of the two methods are now considered in more detail.

5.7 The sample sizes in several SIC Classes (SICs 16, 17, 21, 23, 26 and 33) are less than ten, which is due to the relatively small number of firms in these sectors of industry in the UK from which to sample in the first instance. For these small samples we can be less certain of the accuracy of estimates produced using them than for larger samples. The numbers employed in each of these sectors of industry in the UK, however, are relatively small and the effect on the total UK arisings estimate will not be significant.

5.8 It may be argued that where the confidence interval associated with any estimate based on the survey data *includes* the corresponding estimate based on the disposal plans, the disposal plan figure should be used. There are only six SIC Classes where this could be considered: SICs 34, 36, 43 to 45, 47, 48 and 67. However, the reason that a substitution between the two estimates can be considered in these cases is because they are sufficiently close to one another that one figure falls within the confidence interval of the other. The sample sizes for these groups are large enough for the confidence intervals to be relatively small. There would therefore be very little to be gained from adopting this approach.

5.9 In attempting to draw to a conclusion which of the two methods provides the more accurate reflection of annual industrial waste arisings, we must take into account the dramatic changes in the UK's industrial base over the period of time spanned by the disposal plan and survey data.

5.10 The waste disposal plans containing data of use to this study were published between 1977 and 1989. During this time, the UK has witnessed a decline in its manufacturing industries and growth in its service industries. Between 1981 and 1991, employment in manufacturing industries fell by around 20% from 6.4 million to 5.1 million. In the service sector on the other hand, employment rose by approximately 25% from 10.1 million to 12.7 million.

5.11 The industrial survey data used in the second method were collected during the late 1980s and early 1990s. It could therefore be argued that estimates made using these data sets will be more likely to reflect the result of the industrial changes which occurred during the late 1970s and early 1980s than the aggregated disposal plan data.

5.12 Changes in employment levels within manufacturing and service industries may therefore go some way to explain the differences between the two sets of estimates. However, there is still a large discrepancy which cannot be adequately explained. There is a clear need for further investigation into this issue although this is beyond the remit of this project.

5.13 On balance, however, using the survey data has fewer disadvantages than using the Waste Disposal Plan data, mainly due to the changes in industry that have occurred since the 1970s. In addition, the errors associated with the estimates are far more explicit than the Waste Disposal Plan data and in most cases, proved not to be overly large (see Table A1.7). Nevertheless, the Waste Disposal Plan data cannot be ignored. There was therefore no alternative but to use both sets, acting as independent estimates, for predicting likely trends.

6 THE POSSIBLE IMPACT ON INDUSTRY OF AN INCREASE IN LANDFILL PRICE

Introduction

6.1 In this section, we move from estimates of the quantities of industrial and commercial waste going to landfill in the UK to the final and more fundamental aspect of the project - to estimate the potential impact on industry of an increase in the cost of landfill. For the purposes of this project, a fixed increase of £5 per tonne of waste landfilled was assumed.

Costs to Industry

6.2 To estimate the additional costs to industry of a £5 per tonne increase in landfill costs, the waste arisings figures for each industry sector were multiplied by the cost of the increase expressed in £ per tonne and converted into millions of pounds. Total cost to industry is therefore estimated at around £366 million using the survey data and at £416 million using the Waste Disposal Plan data.

6.3 In order to determine which industries would be the most heavily affected by the levy, the cost was also represented in terms of proportion of gross output. Information on gross output was obtained from the Census of Production. This census only covers manufacturing industry, however; no comparable data could be found for construction or commerce. As Table 6.1 shows, these are generally range between 0.01% and 1% of annual gross output, the average being around 0.1%.

Summary and Results

6.4 Table 6.1 shows the combined results of the calculations described above. An explanation of the source of the data included can be found in Appendix 3.

Table 6.1: Estimated Impact of a £5 increase in Landfill Price on Industry and Commerce

INDUSTRY GROUP	ANNUAL OUTPUT (£ MILLION)	COST OF A £5 INCREASE IN LANDFILL PRICE (£ MILLION)		COST OF PRICE INCREASE AS % OF OUTPUT	
		Survey data	WDP data	Survey data	WDP data
Coal extraction; coke ovens; extraction of oil and gas etc	34728.0	4.5	13.0	0.01%	0.04%
Prod and dist of electricity, gas and other forms of energy	38447.5	5.9	19.2	0.02%	0.05%
Water supply industry	3014.2	0.3	4.7	0.01%	0.16%
Extraction and preparation of metalliferous mineral ores	MISSING	MISSING	MISSING	MISSING	MISSING
Metal manufacturing	12700.4	8.5	41.7	0.07%	0.33%
Extraction of minerals not elsewhere specified	697.7	not sig	8.6	not sig	1.23%
Manufacture of non-metallic mineral products	11196.0	10.5	53.1	0.09%	0.47%
Chemical industry	33553.1	10.7	93.9	0.03%	0.28%
Production of man-made fibres	1009.7	not sig	1.8	not sig	0.18%
Manufacture of metal goods not elsewhere specified	14400.4	9.5	3.1	0.07%	0.02%
Mechanical engineering	31269.7	10.1	7.6	0.03%	0.02%
Manufacture of office machinery & data processing equip.	8289.6	not sig	0.8	not sig	0.01%
Electrical and electronic engineering	25706.4	6.4	5.6	0.02%	0.02%
Manufacture of motor vehicles and parts thereof	21052.8	6.9	2.5	0.03%	0.01%
Manufacture of other transport equipment	15545.1	3.4	2.5	0.02%	0.02%
Instrument engineering	3927.7	2.4	0.9	0.06%	0.02%
Food, drink and tobacco manufacturing industries	60237.0	27.6	9.5	0.05%	0.02%
Textiles, leather and leather goods, footwear and clothing	15348.2	6.0	7.7	0.04%	0.05%
Timber and wooden furniture industries	9463.6	11.9	3.8	0.13%	0.04%
Man. of paper and paper products; printing and publishing	28356.5	8.6	8.1	0.03%	0.03%
Processing of rubber and plastics	12886.4	4.1	3.6	0.03%	0.03%
Other manufacturing industries	3268.5	0.8	1.2	0.02%	0.04%
Construction	73000.0	59.4	59.4	0.08%	0.08%
Wholesale distribution	MISSING	18.8	5.9	MISSING	MISSING
Dealing in scrap and waste materials	MISSING	2.5	2.5	MISSING	MISSING
Commission agents	MISSING	MISSING	0.2	MISSING	MISSING
Retail distribution	MISSING	45.8	15.7	MISSING	MISSING
Hotels and catering	MISSING	16.5	8.1	MISSING	MISSING
Repair of consumer goods and vehicles	MISSING	1.7	1.3	MISSING	MISSING
Transport and communication	MISSING	12.7	6.3	MISSING	MISSING
Banking, finance, insurance, business services, leasing	MISSING	25.5	4.4	MISSING	MISSING
Other services	MISSING	45.0	19.6	MISSING	MISSING
All economic activities	MISSING	366.0	416.3	MISSING	MISSING

34

7 ESTIMATING LIKELY FUTURE TRENDS

Introduction

7.1 In order to estimate the future impact of any increase in the cost of landfill on UK businesses, forecasts must be made of the likely quantities of industrial and commercial waste arising and being disposed of to landfill for the year 2000.

7.2 Making projections of future waste arisings is extremely problematic, mainly due to a general lack of understanding of the factors which cause waste to be generated.

7.3 The Waste Disposal Plans produced by Waste Regulation and Disposal Authorities under the Control of Pollution Act have to include a section on likely future conditions which requires that projections of the types and quantities of waste arising are produced. No guidance on the methods to be used in such a procedure is given in Waste Management Paper 2, however, and partly as a consequence, authorities have used widely differing methods. The table below, reproduced from M.E.L Research's Review and Appraisal of English Waste Disposal Plans (Volume 1: Overview and Appraisal)[16], demonstrates the range of techniques employed:

TABLE C1: INDUSTRIAL WASTE FORECASTS		
Factors Taken into Account	**Number of Plans**	**Authorities**
Unclear - 'Assumed' to remain the same	8	Cheshire, Hereford & Worcester, Lancashire, Somerset, Barnsley, Surrey, West Sussex, Wiltshire
Employment changes	3	Avon, Cambridgeshire, Derbyshire*, Leicestershire*, West Midlands*
Industrial growth/decline	5	Cornwall, Sheffield, Humberside, Leicestershire*, West Midlands*
Past experience	2	Devon, Norfolk
Population	1	Buckinghamshire
Recycling trends	1	Cumbria
Changes in output	1	Derbyshire*
Survey trends analysis	1	Gloucestershire
Range of assumptions	1	Hampshire
Changes in the structure of employment	2	Kent*, West Yorkshire
New industrial developments	1	Kent*
Past trends	1	Suffolk
Increases in road building	1	Shropshire
Impact of waste minimisation	1	West Midlands*
Unclear	7	Bedfordshire, Berkshire, East Sussex, West London, Greater Manchester, Lincolnshire, Northumberland, Nottinghamshire

Authorities Not Forecasting the Category:

Cleveland, Durham, Essex, Western Riverside, Central London, Hertfordshire, Isle of Wight, Merseyside, Northamptonshire, North Yorkshire, Oxfordshire, Rotherham, Staffordshire, Warwickshire

Methods Used in This Project

7.4 As the principal assumption used throughout the project is that rates of waste generation are related to employment levels, changes in employment is the obvious indicator to use for forecasting changes in waste generation.

7.5 However, some work has also been undertaken by SERPLAN (South East Region Planning Conference) on quantities of waste expected to arise and require disposal in the South East region between 1992 and 2005. While the principal estimator of future quantities should be employment, the SERPLAN data have been included here for comparison purposes. It should be noted that SERPLAN projections are based on population increases and are not therefore strictly compatible; they have been included here as one of the few projections available.

SERPLAN Data

7.6 SERPLAN carries out biennial surveys of waste arisings and void space for landfill in the region. A draft report currently being circulated for consultation *Numerical Guidance: Waste Disposal Options for the South East: Interim Report of the Waste Disposal Working Party*[17] contains waste predictions for 2005 under three scenarios:

1. no change in the level of arisings
2. increased recycling and incineration of waste according to European and UK policy
3. the concept of using landfill as a last resort being achieved

7.7 SERPLAN lists three compositional categories of waste - A, B and C which relate broadly to the biodegradability of the waste when landfilled. For the purposes of this project Category A would equate roughly to construction waste, Category B to industrial and commercial waste and Category C to household waste.

7.8 SERPLAN predicts an increase of around 26% by the year 2005 for Category A waste (construction-type waste) and a 1% increase in Category B arisings under the 'no change' scenario. Under the increases recycling and incineration option, a prediction of a 4% increase in Category A is made and 1% in Category B while under the landfill as a last resort option decreases of 13% and 18% are predicted.

Employment as Estimator of Future Trends

7.9 Two sources of information were found which provide predictions of employment levels by industry group for 2000 although both sources derive from one organisation - The Institute for Employment Research based at Warwick University. The first source is a report produced by the Skills and Enterprise Network entitled *Labour Market and Skills Trends 1994/5*[18] while the second is a report is published by the Institute for Employment Research itself and is entitled *Review of Economy and Employment*[19]. The two sources have been combined, the second supplementing the first where more detail is available on certain industry groups, to create the following table of estimates of changes in employment in the year 2000 compared to a base line year of 1991 (which is also the year of the data on waste arisings included in this report due to the use made throughout of 1991 employment data):

Table 7.1: Changes in Waste Generation Expected to have Occurred by 2000

Standard Industrial Classification 1980		% change 1991 - 2000
11 - 17	Primary and utilities	-24%
21 - 49	Manufacturing	-12%
50	Construction	-3%
61, 64/65	Wholesale & Retail Distribution	+1%
62, 63, 67	Other Distribution; Repairs	-0.5%
66	Hotels and Catering	+6.5%
71 -79	Transport and Communication	-8%
81 - 85	Banking, Finance, Insurance etc	+16%
91 - 98	Other services	+8%
11 - 98	ALL SECTORS	+2%

7.10 These factors were then applied to the figures for waste arising (both survey data estimates and Waste Disposal Plan estimates) to derive two estimates of the likely future quantities of waste arising by industry sector. An identical approach was adopted for estimating future quantities of waste going for landfilling; that is, no account has been taken of a possible decrease in waste going to landfill through the introduction of policies aimed at diverting waste away from this method of disposal or of any increase in waste minimisation or recycling.

7.11 The dramatic decline in employment, and hence waste generation, expected to occur in primary and manufacturing industry is reflected in the estimated costs of a nominal £5 increase in landfill price in the year 2000 as presented in Table 7.2.

7.12 When compared to the present estimates as presented in Table 6.1, the cost to the food, drink and tobacco manufacturing industry (SIC Classes 41/42) as estimated from the survey data, for example, is expected to fall from £28 million to £24 million while the costs to banking, finance, insurance, business services and leasing (SIC Classes 81-85) will rise from £25 million to £30 million. Overall, the total costs to industry and commerce fall by 3% from £366 million to £355 million using the survey data and by 9% from £416 to £378 million using the Waste Disposal Plan data by the year 2000. This is due to the predicted decline in employment within the construction and manufacturing industries. The relative costs expressed as a percentage of annual gross output are the same as those presented in Table 6.1 since gross output figures have also been indexed using projected changes in employment. It is likely that there is a far more complex relationship between gross output levels and employment which may lead to different relative values being produced, however.

Table 7.2: Estimated Impact on Industry of a £5 Increase in Landfill Price (Year 2000)

INDUSTRY GROUP	PROJECTED OUTPUT (£ MILLION)	COST OF A £5 INCREASE IN LANDFILL PRICE (£ MILLION)		COST OF PRICE INCREASE AS % OF PROJECTED OUTPUT	
		Survey data	WDP data	Survey data	WDP data
Coal extraction; coke ovens; extraction of oil and gas etc	26,393	3.4	9.9	0.01%	0.04%
Prod and dist of electricity, gas and other forms of energy	29,220	4.5	14.6	0.02%	0.05%
Water supply industry	2,291	0.2	3.6	0.01%	0.16%
Extraction and preparation of metalliferous mineral ores	MISSING	MISSING	MISSING	MISSING	MISSING
Metal manufacturing	11,176	7.5	36.7	0.07%	0.33%
Extraction of minerals not elsewhere specified	614	not sig	7.6	not sig	1.23%
Manufacture of non-metallic mineral products	9,852	9.2	46.7	0.09%	0.47%
Chemical industry	29,527	9.4	82.6	0.03%	0.28%
Production of man-made fibres	889	not sig	1.6	not sig	0.18%
Manufacture of metal goods not elsewhere specified	12,672	8.4	2.7	0.07%	0.02%
Mechanical engineering	27,517	8.9	6.7	0.03%	0.02%
Manufacture of office machinery & data processing equip.	7,295	not sig	0.7	not sig	0.01%
Electrical and electronic engineering	22,622	5.6	4.9	0.02%	0.02%
Manufacture of motor vehicles and parts thereof	18,526	6.1	2.2	0.03%	0.01%
Manufacture of other transport equipment	13,680	3.0	2.2	0.02%	0.02%
Instrument engineering	3,456	2.2	0.8	0.06%	0.02%
Food, drink and tobacco manufacturing industries	53,009	24.2	8.4	0.05%	0.02%
Textiles, leather and leather goods, footwear and clothing	13,506	5.3	6.8	0.04%	0.05%
Timber and wooden furniture industries	8,328	10.5	3.3	0.13%	0.04%
Man. of paper and paper products; printing and publishing	24,954	7.6	7.2	0.03%	0.03%
Processing of rubber and plastics	11,340	3.6	3.2	0.03%	0.03%
Other manufacturing industries	2,876	0.7	1.1	0.02%	0.04%
Construction	70,810	57.6	57.6	0.08%	0.08%
Wholesale distribution	MISSING	19.9	6.0	MISSING	MISSING
Dealing in scrap and waste materials	MISSING	2.5	2.5	MISSING	MISSING
Commission agents	MISSING	MISSING	0.2	MISSING	MISSING
Retail distribution	MISSING	46.3	15.8	MISSING	MISSING
Hotels and catering	MISSING	17.5	8.6	MISSING	MISSING
Repair of consumer goods and vehicles	MISSING	1.7	1.3	MISSING	MISSING
Transport and communication	MISSING	11.7	5.8	MISSING	MISSING
Banking, finance, insurance, business services, leasing	MISSING	29.6	5.1	MISSING	MISSING
Other services	MISSING	48.6	21.2	MISSING	MISSING
All economic activities	**MISSING**	**354.8**	**377.5**	**MISSING**	**MISSING**

8 ESTIMATING WASTE COMPOSITION

Introduction

8.1   Information on the composition of waste is relevant to the project as landfill price generally increases proportional to the difficulty of the waste in terms of its reactivity. Special waste, for example, attracts a far higher charge than inert waste. There are two principal sources of information available in the composition of waste being disposed of to landfill. These are:

1.   Waste Disposal Plan data
2.   Raw survey data

8.2   Both sets were initially examined for suitability and it was concluded that the distribution of the composition of waste varied dramatically from county to county. For this reason, it was decided not to use the raw survey data from which suitable data were only available for one geographical area but rather to use the Waste Disposal Plan data.

8.3   Waste Regulation Authorities have on the whole used the Department of the Environment coding system to classify the composition of wastes. As these do not neatly fall into the categories of inert and non-inert, the table below describes waste according to the DoE system. It should be noted that construction waste is classified as S93 and therefore falls within the large Miscellaneous category (S) while metal will fall within category J and glass (S90) again within S. It was not possible to determine the quantity of inert waste with any accuracy as much of the waste may cross into the landfill site as a mixed load and to quote proportions of Categories S and J would therefore be misleading.

Composition of waste being landfilled in the UK

8.4   Table 8.1 below shows the range of values in the UK from the five Waste Disposal Plans which provided data. The last two columns have been calculated by multiplying the median percentage composition by the estimated quantities landfilled per annum in the UK using the two methods.

Table 8.1: Distribution of composition in the UK (WDP data)

DoE Waste Category	Range (%)	Median (%)	Quantity landfilled (survey data) ('000 tonnes)	Quantity landfilled (WDP data) ('000 tonnes)
A - Inorganic Acids	0 - 2	<1	not sig	not sig
B - Organic Acids	0	<1	not sig	not sig
C - Alkalis	0 - 2	<1	not sig	not sig
D - Toxic Metal Compounds	0 - 4	1	732	833
E - Non- Toxic Metal Compounds	0 - 1	<1	not sig	not sig
F - Metals (Elemental)	0 - 19	1	732	833
G - Metal Oxides	0	<1	not sig	not sig
H - Inorganic Compounds	0 - 1	<1	not sig	not sig
J - Other Inorganic Compounds	17 - 59	44	32,215	36,637
K - Organic Compounds	0	<1	not sig	not sig
L - Polymeric Materials	1 - 3	1	732	833
M - Fuels, Oils and Greases	0 - 4	2	1,464	1,665
N - Fine Chemicals etc	0	<1	not sig	not sig
P - Miscellaneous Chemical Waste	0 - 1	<1	not sig	not sig
Q - Filter Materials etc	0 - 27	2	1,464	1,665
R - Interceptor Wastes	1 - 4	2	1,464	1,665
S - Miscellaneous Waste	6 - 48	38	27,822	31,640
T - Animal and Food Waste	3 - 48	9	6,589	7,494
U - Clinical Waste	0 - 6	<1	not sig	not sig
		100%	73,214	83,265

8.5 Most of the waste falls within categories J (Other Inorganic Compounds) and S (Miscellaneous Waste). These will cover materials such as metal, paper, cardboard and inert and non-inert construction waste. There is clearly need for further research if information is required in any more detail than that provided here.

9 ESTIMATING THE PRESENT COSTS OF LANDFILL

Introduction

9.1   There is very little information on the costs of waste disposal to industry. This is particularly problematic at the current time as disposal sites try to beat the new licensing regulations by reducing prices considerably. In summary, prices are fluctuating to such an extent that it is extremely difficult to provide any reliable figures.

9.2   In addition, the price paid by industry for the disposal of waste is generally based on contracts which are based on the price of lifting a container rather than the weight of the waste being removed. Transport costs are estimated according to the size of the vehicle while the cost at the landfill gate may be based on the number and size of containers or the number of axles the vehicle has or on the weight of the waste.

Sources of data used in the project

9.3   Only three published sources of data were found which related specifically to the costs of waste disposal. These are the Coopers and Lybrand report on Landfill Costs and Prices, an article that appeared in Industrial Waste Management in May 1992 and the Howard Humphreys report on construction and demolition waste.

9.4   Data from the Coopers and Lybrand report only covers disposal costs of domestic and commercial waste to landfill and states that the cost of disposal of this waste at the point of arising is between £5 and £30 per tonne, depending on the area of the country.

9.5   The article from Industrial Waste Management does not state specific prices as costs are based on the size of containers used; the information of relevance is reproduced over the page for completeness only.

Typical Charges for Commercial and Industrial Wastes

Collection and Disposal Charges

Vehicle System	Container	Payload	Typical Charge
Rolonoff	30m	5 - 6t	£90 - £150 per lift
FEL	6 - 8m	1 - 1.5t	£20 - £25 per lift
REL	9m	1.5 - 2t	£30 per lift
Skip	9m	1.5 - 2t	£65 - £70 per lift
Mini-skip	2 - 3m	0.3 - 0.5t	£25 - £28 per lift
Asbestos wastes	special	1t	£125 - £150 per lift

Landfill Disposal Charges WDA Sites Midlands

General commercial and industrial waste	£8 - £10 per t
Gully wastes, sweepings	£8 - £10 per t
Scrap metal fragmentiser waste	£8 - £10 per t
Hard core, foundry sand, soil	£5 - £8 per t
Bonded asbestos	£45 per t
Food waste	£20 per t
Sewage sludge	£20 per t

Note: This data is compiled from a number of leading companies and WDA in the Midlands in 1991. Contracted prices may depend on size of the order and other commercial factors.

9.6 In Appendix D of their draft report, Howard Humphreys cite some ranges of costs for construction waste at the landfill gate, varying according to the geographical location of the site. For inert construction waste these range between £1 and £3 per tonne while for construction waste containing non-inert materials such as wood or cardboard, the costs ranged between £3 and £16 per tonne. However, transport and other costs would also need to be taken into account if the true cost to industry was to be derived. Information on these aspects of a contract for waste removal could not be easily uncovered. Confidentiality of information is a particular problem in this respect.

9.7 Aspinwall and Company have estimated that costs of disposal range from £500 million to £1000 million nationally. This would equate to a cost of between £6.50 - £13 per tonne to each business based on the data published earlier in this report.

9.8 In addition, the British Scrap Federation stated that the waste their members "liberate to landfill" costs £11 per tonne at the landfill gate.

9.9 Estimates of the costs to businesses can therefore be summarised as follows.

Howard Humphreys estimate for construction and demolition wastes (excluding transport costs)	£1 - £3 per tonne (inert) £3 - £16 per tonne (contaminated)
British Scrap Federation estimate (excluding transport costs)	£11 per tonne (average)
Estimate derived from an Aspinwall and Company estimate	£6.50 - £13 per tonne
Coopers and Lybrand estimate for household and commercial waste	£5 - £30 per tonne
KPMG Management Consulting estimate for 1990 annual turnover from landfill of £950 million divided by best estimate of amount of waste landfilled	About £10 per tonne (average for all controlled waste)

Conclusions

9.10 It can therefore be concluded that although accurate figures on the costs of landfill to businesses are not available, these are likely to fall within the range of £1 to £30 per tonne (except for certain special wastes) with an overall average of around £10 per tonne. Costs are partly dependant on the type of material being landfilled and partly dependant on the area of the country within which the landfill site is situated. Further research would be needed if estimates of costs to each sector of industry were to be required.

10 REFERENCES

1   **Standard Industrial Classification 1980**
     (CSO: HMSO)

2   **Census of Employment 1991: Regions in GB**
     Census of Employment 1991: Local area in GB
     (CSO)

3   **Census of Production 1991**
     (CSO)

4   **Economic Instruments and Recovery of Resources from Waste**
     Environmental Resources Ltd (HMSO 1992)

5   **Landfill Costs and Prices: Correcting Possible Market Distortions**
     (Coopers and Lybrand: HMSO 1993)

6   **Externalities from Landfill and Incineration**
     (CSERGE, Warren Spring Laboratory and EFTEL: HMSO 1993)

7   **The eleventh report of the Royal Commission on Environmental Pollution**
     (Managing Waste: The Duty of Care)
     (HMSO 1985)

8   **Waste Management Paper 2: Waste Disposal Surveys**
     (HMSO 1976)

9   **Waste Management Paper 3: Guideline for the Preparation of a Waste**
     Disposal Plan
     (HMSO 1976)

10   **General Industrial Waste Programme: Development of a Sampling**
     Methodology
     Aspinwall and Company (1993)

11   A R Tron (1978) **The production of solid industrial and commercial wastes**
     in Britain and their potential recovery (unpublished report, Warren Spring
     Laboratory)

12   Ader & Buck (1983) **Refuse as a fuel - resource mapping** (report of a study
     conducted in behalf of the Energy Technology Support Unit)

13   **Commentary on the Techniques for Determining Arisings of Industrial**
     Solid Wastes
     Aspinwall and Company (1990)

14   **Recycling of Commercial Waste in Sheffield**
     M.E.L Research Report 91/02

15   **Commercial Waste: Arisings, Recycling and Waste Management Practices**
     in the West Midlands County 1993
     M.E.L Research report on behalf of the West Midlands Waste Management
     Coordinating Authority (unpublished)

16   **Review and Appraisal of English Waste Disposal Plans (Volume 1:**
     Overview and Appraisal)
     M.E.L Research report 93/401 (CWM 053/92)

17   **Numerical Guidance: Waste Disposal Options for the South East: Interim**
     Report of the Waste Disposal Working Party
     SERPLAN Draft Report for Consultation

18   **Labour Market and Skill Trends 1994/5**
      Skills and Enterprise Network 1993

19   **Review of Economy and Employment**
      Institute of Employment Research

20   **The West Midlands Waste Management Coordinating Authority -
      Industrial Waste Survey**
      M.E.L Research Report 94/07B

21   J Aitchison and J A C Brown **The Log normal Distribution**
      Cambridge University Press (1957)

APPENDICES

APPENDIX 1

DETAILED METHODOLOGY FOR CALCULATING
TOTAL WASTE ARISINGS

A1 DETAILED METHODOLOGY FOR CALCULATING TOTAL WASTE ARISINGS

Introduction

A1.1 Waste arising refers to all waste being produced by, in this case, industry and commerce (including the construction industry). This includes waste recycled, although not waste reused internally by companies. It specifically excludes waste arising from agriculture, forestry and fishing activities (Division 0) as these are not currently classified as controlled wastes and, as a result, the data available on quantities are unreliable. In any case, it is likely that only a very small proportion of agricultural waste is disposed of to licensed landfill sites.

A1.2 This chapter explains how estimates have been derived from available data on industrial and commercial waste arising in the UK. Two key sources of data were used to separately produce estimates, slightly different estimation methods being used for each source. These are:

1. Waste Disposal Plans
2. Raw data from surveys carried out by M.E.L Research and Waste Disposal and Regulation Authorities

A1.3 Estimates produced using the two sources of data are presented at the end of the chapter in Table A1.9.

A1.4 In addition, estimates produced from other published sources and data obtained from other European member states have been presented for comparative purposes.

Background to the Data Used in the Project

Methodology

A.15 Data from all of the sources above were produced using the same basic methodology. The most commonly used approach to calculating waste arisings is a survey of a producer's premises. This study uses the data obtained through surveys carried out by Waste Disposal and Regulation Authorities in England who have generally followed the methodology suggested in Waste Management Paper 2. In summary, this involves a census of companies employing more than 1000 staff and a sample survey of the remainder.

Sources of Error

A1.6 There are several kinds of error that are likely to be present in these surveys. These include:

1. **Measurement error**

   Error is present in surveys where the respondent is asked to state the quantity and composition of the waste produced in the company. This error is reduced by a personal visit to the premises by the survey officer although there is bound to be some degree of error in any estimation process. As waste is not generally weighed on the premises, quantities will be estimates based on statements made by respondents about the capacity of the container, the frequency with which it is collected, how full the container usually is on collection and what waste materials are put into it.

2. **Conversion error**

   As estimates obtained from surveys are generally in volumetric units while the data are required in tonnes, some form of conversion must be undertaken. Waste Disposal and Regulation Authorities generally rely on volume to weight conversion factors. There is no set of validated, national conversion factors and over the years authorities have developed their own. The error caused by inaccurate and non-standard volume to weight conversion factors has long been recognised but has never been fully assessed.

3. **Sampling error**

   When a sample mean is used to estimate a population mean, different estimates will be obtained from different samples. This error is measurable and can be expressed in a confidence interval. However, few of the results of surveys used in this study have included confidence limits and it is not possible to determine these from aggregated data sets.

4. **Coverage error**

   The most commonly used information for selecting a sample of firms is the biennial Census of Employment. This survey only includes a sample of firms itself, however, and therefore may be unrepresentative of the area in question. In addition, the most recent results are often several years out of date such that employment data from firms that have only just started up will be omitted and that from firms that have closed may be included.

5. **Grossing-up error**

   As mentioned elsewhere in this report, the tonnes per employee per annum parameter has been used in the majority of surveys as the means of estimating waste arisings for companies that were not included in the sample. M.E.L Research, in work undertaken on behalf of the West Midlands Waste Management Coordinating Authority[20], has shown that there is a weak correlation between these two variables in many of the industry sectors and the accuracy of the results obtained through such a method should be questioned. Gross output is one of the more easily obtained of the many other proxy variables that have been suggested could be used for such a purpose. However, this is only available on a national level for manufacturing industry and is generally regarded as commercially confidential on the level of individual firms. There is therefore currently no other practical alternative to using employment as the proxy variable.

6. The use of the average tonnes per employee figure for grossing up purposes

Waste generation shows a highly positively skewed distribution, with the vast majority of firms producing small amounts of waste while a few firms produce large quantities. This has implications for determining the average value of tonnes per employee per annum within each sector of industry since the distribution of the sample mean has a high variance which causes it sometimes to seriously overestimate the population mean and at other times to underestimate the population mean. It is very likely that the surveys used in this study have made no attempt to correct for this observation. Further detail on suitable correction methods is included in sections A1.35 to A1.37.

Methodology Used in this Project

A1.7   The object of this part of the study was to derive an estimate for total industrial and commercial waste arising in the UK. Each source of secondary data was therefore examined for useful data, the most important factor being that a breakdown of waste arising within each sector of industry be available.

Data from the Waste Disposal Plans

A1.8   Each Waste Disposal Plan was systematically reviewed and relevant data were extracted. These related to four parameters:

1. Waste arising within each 1968 Standard Industrial Classification Order
2. Waste arising within each 1980 Standard Industrial Classification Division
3. Composition of non-special industrial and commercial waste by Department of the Environment code
4. Composition of special waste by Department of the Environment code

A1.9   This appendix deals with the procedure for estimating total waste arisings by industry of origin; composition is dealt with in Chapter 8.

A1.10 The estimation process consisted of five stages, as follows:

1. Conversion of data in 1968 Standard Industrial Classification format to 1980 Standard Industrial Classification Divisions
2. Filling in the gaps for counties and districts with no data to produce regional and national estimates
3. Estimation for areas not covered by the Waste Disposal Plans (Scotland, Wales and Northern Ireland)
4. Disaggregation from SIC Division to SIC Class
5. Production of total quantities by grouped SIC Classes for the UK

A1.11 Each stage of the estimation process listed above is described in detail below.

Stage 1: SIC Conversion

A1.12 It was agreed at the start of the project that 1980 Standard Industrial Classification should be used for the project so a conversion procedure had to be undertaken for data in 1968 format. 1968 Orders are broken down into Minimum List Headings (MLHs) which roughly correspond to 1980 Classes, several of which comprise a 1980 Division. The following diagram shows how this transposition is possible.

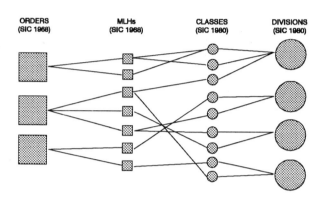

A1.13 The conversion assumptions are listed below:

Standard Industrial Classification (1980) Divisions	Standard Industrial Classification (1968) Orders
1 Energy and water supply industries	II (MLH 101 AND 104), IV, XXI
2 Extraction of minerals and ores other than fuels; manufacture of metals, mineral products and chemicals	II (MLH 102, 103, 109), V, VI, XVI
3 Metal goods, engineering and vehicle manufacture industries	VII - XII
4 Other manufacturing industries	III, XIII - XV
5 Construction	XX
6 Distribution, hotels and catering; repairs	XXIII, XXVI (MLH 884-888, 894, 895)
7 Transport and communication	XXII
8 Banking, finance, insurance, business services and leasing	XXIV, XXV (MLH 871, 873, 879)
9 Other services	XXV (Remainder), XXVI (Remainder), XXVII

Source: Standard Industrial Classification 1980 (CSO; HMSO)

A1.14 As the table above shows, there were several Orders that did not fall neatly into the 1980 classification, some Minimum List Headings (MLHs) being in one Division and some in another. In order to convert the data in SIC 1968 format into SIC 1980 format, a means of apportioning SIC Orders II, XXV and XXVI had to be devised. One possibility was to apportion MLHs according to occurrence. Two of the five MLHs within Order II, for example, fall to Division 1 while the remaining three fall to Division 2, so two fifths of the quantity of waste arising within Order II could be assigned to Division 1 and three fifths to Division 2. This approach was not adopted, however, as takes no account of the distribution of industry within Order II. Instead a method based on employment was used. Although no employment data are available for the 1968 classification, MLHs map roughly to 1980 SIC Classes. Once this mapping was completed, employment within each of the Classes was used to apportion the waste. The results are as follows:

Order II

1968 MLH	1980 Class	Employment GB (1991)	1980 Division	% Attributable
101	11	72,200	1	80
104	13	19,000		
102 103 109	23	22,500	2	20

Order XXV

1968 MLH	1980 Class	Employment GB (1991)	1980 Division	% Attributable
871 873 879	83	1,310,000	8	27
874	91	1,142,600	9	73
872	93	1,477,900		
876	94	80,400		
875	96	767,900		

Order XXVI

1968 MLH	1980 Class	Employment GB (1991)	1980 Division	% Attributable
881 882 883	97	435,800	9	34
889 892 893 899	98	164,800		
884 885 886 887 888	66	1,014,000	6	66
894 895	67	165,300		

A1.15 This conversion procedure had to be undertaken for a total of 19 Waste Disposal Plans.

A1.16 Once all the Waste Disposal Plan data were in a compatible format (Standard Industrial Classification 1980), a table was produced showing the figures provided by each plan. The results are shown in Table A1.1.

DETAILED METHODOLOGY FOR CALCULATING TOTAL WASTE ARISINGS

Table A1.1: Data Available from Waste Disposal Plans

COUNTY	DATE	Standard Industrial Classification 1980									TOTAL ARISINGS
		DIVISION 1	DIVISION 2	DIVISION 3	DIVISION 4	DIVISION 5	DIVISION 6	DIVISION 7	DIVISION 8	DIVISION 9	
SOUTH EAST											
BEDFORDSHIRE	1984	19795	44340	32325	5764	200000	36154	8700	6232	19814	373124
BERKSHIRE											
BUCKINGHAMSHIRE	1978	22351	99093	47073	17431	702130	15542	1978	2990	9703	918291
EAST SUSSEX											
ESSEX											
WEST LONDON	1989	27812	24664	237525	172189	28897	163748	68589	52154	218770	994348
EAST LONDON	1980	5	71004	53534	179006	35652	140130	61207	47216	48525	636279
CENTRAL LONDON											
SE LONDON											
S LONDON											
N LONDON											
BEXLEY											
WESTERN RIVERSIDE											
HAMPSHIRE											
HERTFORDSHIRE											
ISLE OF WIGHT											
KENT	1977	1101171	654960	88233	50539		226245	32124	10683	65120	
OXFORDSHIRE											
SURREY											
WEST SUSSEX											
EAST ANGLIA											
CAMBRIDGESHIRE	1979	290107	115416	92082	374804	92888	50972	12156	56505	91176	1176106
NORFOLK											
SUFFOLK	1984	92683	132693	98703	478488	22240	45648	19777	6376	24362	920970
SOUTH WEST											
AVON	1988	10531	301433	64060	171011	860000	152594	66404	10645	47494	1684172
CORNWALL	1978	5892	13064	231722	278001	31	1225			1149	
DEVON	1979	22000	255500	73000	56000	550000					
DORSET											
GLOUCESTERSHIRE	1978	32	65588	52475	20159	433780					
SOMERSET		5714	25320	19385	67035	218991	51010	10166	2727	12626	412974
WILTSHIRE											

Table A1.1 (cont): Data Available From Waste Disposal Plans

		DIVISION 1	DIVISION 2	DIVISION 3	DIVISION 4	DIVISION 5	DIVISION 6	DIVISION 7	DIVISION 8	DIVISION 9	TOTAL ARISINGS
WEST MIDLANDS											
HEREFORD & WORCS	1983	123	54501	118437	132467	387974					
SHROPSHIRE	1987		13950	72080	247530						
STAFFORDSHIRE		1496	114425	52343	212763			2532			
WARWICKSHIRE	1984		112405	52838	10127						
WEST MIDLANDS							250700	24900	27400	194900	
EAST MIDLANDS											
DERBYSHIRE		51112	741270	86339	58663						
LEICESTERSHIRE	1981	6733	62099	76001	73926		157964	56101	1611	21336	
LINCOLNSHIRE	1986	5738	41838	45850	194048	400000	82160	12194	1622	5217	
NORTHAMPTONSHIRE	1979		307240	47270	99740		39754	12640	6094	22402	788667
NOTTINGHAMSHIRE											
YORKS & HUMBS											
HUMBERSIDE	1985										
NORTH YORKSHIRE			18600	7260	33150	1000000					
SHEFFIELD	1988		208346	187128	78543		116991	6863	4872	79732	
DONCASTER	1988	387000	77000	87000	40000						
ROTHERHAM											
BARNSLEY											
WEST YORKSHIRE	1987	854000	379400	273900	507200	356700	691200	82000	37300	221600	3403300
NORTH WEST											
CHESHIRE	1987	56200	20906100	138900	167300						
GR. MANCHESTER		26558	87306	182448	378586	139391	139391	21499	62273	401629	1439081
LANCASHIRE											
MERSEYSIDE											
NORTHERN											
CLEVELAND	1984	57595	1329145	25812	49705	613000	31464	7892	557	2084	2117254
CUMBRIA											
DURHAM											
NORTHUMBERLAND											
TYNE AND WEAR											

Division 1 Energy and water supply industries
Division 2 Extraction of minerals and ores other than fuels;
            manufacture of metals, mineral products and chemicals
Division 3 Metal goods, engineering and vehicles industries
Division 4 Other manufacturing industries
Division 5 Construction
Division 6 Distribution, hotels and catering; repairs
Division 7 Transport & communication
Division 8 Banking, finance, insurance
            business services and leasing
Division 9 Other services

Stage 2: Filling in the Gaps

A1.17 Table A1.1 shows that forty four of the fifty six Waste Regulation or Disposal Authority plans did not contain a full complement of data. The next stage in the calculation was therefore to fill in the missing data in order to produce estimates of the quantities of waste arising by Standard Industrial Classification Division by region with the aim of deriving a figure for England.

A1.18 Two approaches to filling in missing data were available, both of which were used to derive estimates of industrial and commercial waste arising by industry group (SIC Division) in England. The first approach is to estimate for each region and then add the results together while the second approach by-passes the regional estimates using all known arisings figures to estimate for the whole of England. Table A1.2 shows the results of each method.

A1.19 Firstly, counties and districts were grouped into regions for the purposes of calculating an estimate of waste arising within each industry sector within each region. Census of Employment data were applied to the known waste arisings to calculate a tonnes per employee figure for each SIC Division for each region. This factor was then multiplied by the number of employees within each SIC Division within each region for which data were *not* available (represented by the grey areas in Table A1.1). By combining the total known waste with the total waste estimated for the grey areas, a regional total of waste arising within each SIC Division within each region was derived. The calculation procedure is summarised below:

A Known waste arising for each SIC Division within each region
B Number of employees producing the known waste (1991)
C Tonnes of waste per employee (A/B)
D Number of employees producing the unknown quantity of waste within each SIC Division in each region (1991)
E Tonnes of waste arising within each SIC Division within each region that was previously not known (C x D)
F Total waste arising within each SIC Division within each region (A+E)

A1.20 Some areas proved to be special cases. While the majority of plans were produced by Waste Regulation and Disposal Authorities based at county level (including the Metropolitan counties of West Yorkshire, West Midlands and Merseyside), some are produced by smaller bodies. The districts of South Yorkshire (Barnsley, Doncaster, Rotherham and Sheffield) chose to retain the responsibility for waste regulation when the metropolitan county was dis-established and are therefore responsible for producing Waste Disposal Plans. Available data therefore are included in Table A1.1 for each of the districts. In Greater Manchester, Wigan chose to retain the responsibility for waste regulation and the production of a Waste Disposal Plan and is therefore included separately. In these cases, employment data were required at district level, a breakdown which is again regarded as confidential. Data are available, however, for *grouped* SIC Divisions at district level (0, 2-4, 5, 6, 7-8 and 9). It was therefore necessary to disaggregate the grouped Divisions. This disaggregation process was undertaken on the assumption that the proportion of waste attributable to each SIC Division within the grouped Divisions for each district is the same as the distribution within the appropriate region as a whole. For example, if in Yorkshire and Humberside, 20% of the employment within the grouped SIC Divisions 2, 3 and 4 is attributable to Division 2, 30% to Division 3 and 50% to Division 4, this was the distribution attributed to Sheffield, Barnsley, Doncaster and Rotherham. Similarly, the distribution of employment in Wigan was assumed to be the same as Greater Manchester as a whole and each of the London Boroughs was assumed to mirror the picture within Greater London. The proportions attributed are listed below:

London Boroughs

Grouped Division	Sic Division	Number of employees in Greater London (1991)	%
2,3,4	2	356,600	10
	3	132,200	37
	4	190,400	53
7,8	7	307,700	30
	8	733,500	70

Districts of South Yorkshire

Grouped Division	Sic Division	Number of employees in South Yorkshire (1991)	%
2,3,4	2	283,100	18
	3	159,700	35
	4	215,100	47
7,8	7	96,400	37
	8	167,600	63

Districts of Greater Manchester

Grouped Division	Sic Division	Number of employees in Greater Manchester (1991)	%
2,3,4	2	91,600	16
	3	240,500	42
	4	244,000	42
7,8	7	139,000	37
	8	241,500	63

A1.21 Thirdly, the survey data contained in the Waste Disposal Plans ranged in date from 1977 to 1989. It is likely that the productivity rates of industries will have changed over this time period such that waste per employee rates will also have altered. The increased use of computer technology is also likely to have had an impact on waste generation rates. It has not been possible to address these issues in this project due to the time scale and the fact that economic indexes on these parameters are not readily available.

A1.22 Fourthly, employment data have been taken from the 1991 Census of Employment while, as mentioned above, the data from the Waste Disposal Plans cover the period between 1977 and 1989. A more accurate approach would have been to use backdated employment data. This proved not to be readily available, however, and the project timescale dictated that 1991 data be used throughout.

A1.23 Fifthly, in some cases data for a region were estimated on the basis of only one figure. Northern region, for example, has data only from Cleveland. This method assumes that observations from Cleveland, in this case, will adequately reflect the rest of the counties in the region. In the absence of any research to prove otherwise, it has been assumed that industries within the same region are more likely to use similar technologies and processes and that it would therefore be more accurate to extrapolate missing data from counties within the same region.

A1.24 The results of this stage in the calculation are shown in Table A1.2. Two separate rows of totals for England are shown, the first of which has been derived by pooling all the data and the second by summing the regional estimates. It is notable that the estimates for England produced by the two different methods are very similar for most SIC Divisions.

Table A1.2: Regional Estimates of Waste Arising by SIC Division (WDP data)

REGION	Standard Industrial Classification (1980) Division								
	1	2	3	4	5	6	7	8	9
GREATER LONDON									
A TOTAL TONNES OF KNOWN WASTE	27,817	95,668	291,059	351,195	64,549	303,878	129,796	99,370	267,295
B TOTAL EMPLOYMENT FOR WHITE AREAS (1991)	6,500	12,550	46,435	66,515	30,500	173,400	62,970	146,930	222,900
C TONNES PER EMPLOYEE FOR THE REGION (A/B)	4.28	7.62	6.27	5.28	2.12	1.75	2.06	0.68	1.20
D TOTAL EMPLOYMENT FOR GREY AREAS (1991)	33,400	23,370	86,469	123,861	87,700	585,700	249,450	582,050	826,000
E TOTAL WASTE FOR GREY AREAS (D x C)	142,937	178,148	541,996	653,978	185,605	1,026,421	514,175	393,645	990,514
F TOTAL WASTE ARISING IN THE REGION (A + E)	170,754	273,816	833,055	1,005,173	250,154	1,330,299	643,971	493,015	1,257,809
SOUTH EAST									
A TOTAL TONNES OF KNOWN WASTE	1,143,317	798,393	167,631	73,734	902,130	277,941	42,802	19,905	94,637
B TOTAL EMPLOYMENT FOR WHITE AREAS (1991)	13,400	28,700	100,800	76,800	16,300	218,300	72,300	115,700	298,600
C TONNES PER EMPLOYEE FOR THE REGION (A/B)	85.32	27.82	1.66	0.96	55.35	1.27	0.59	0.17	0.32
D TOTAL EMPLOYMENT FOR GREY AREAS (1991)	44,000	66,200	301,200	169,100	143,500	706,300	175,700	405,200	947,700
E TOTAL WASTE FOR GREY AREAS (D x C)	3,754,175	1,841,589	500,897	162,349	7,942,065	899,266	104,015	69,711	300,360
F TOTAL WASTE ARISING IN THE REGION (A + E)	4,897,492	2,639,982	668,528	236,083	8,844,195	1,177,207	146,817	89,616	394,997
EAST ANGLIA									
A TOTAL TONNES OF KNOWN WASTE	382,790	248,109	190,785	853,292	115,128	96,620	31,933	62,881	115,538
B TOTAL EMPLOYMENT FOR WHITE AREAS (1991)	8,800	11,900	48,100	53,500	21,700	107,400	39,300	53,100	151,500
C TONNES PER EMPLOYEE FOR THE REGION (A/B)	43.50	20.85	3.97	15.95	5.31	0.90	0.81	1.18	0.76
D TOTAL EMPLOYMENT FOR GREY AREAS (1991)	5,100	4,000	19,600	32,200	11,300	64,300	15,000	30,100	80,900
E TOTAL WASTE FOR GREY AREAS (D x C)	221,844	83,398	77,742	513,570	59,951	57,846	12,188	35,644	61,697
F TOTAL WASTE ARISING IN THE REGION (A + E)	604,634	331,507	268,527	1,366,862	175,079	154,466	44,121	98,525	177,235
SOUTH WEST									
A TOTAL TONNES OF KNOWN WASTE	44,169	660,905	440,642	592,206	2,062,802	204,829	76,570	13,372	61,269
B TOTAL EMPLOYMENT FOR WHITE AREAS (1991)	22,300	26,000	122,600	97,200	49,900	167,200	31,600	75,800	286,200
C TONNES PER EMPLOYEE FOR THE REGION (A/B)	1.98	25.42	3.59	6.09	41.34	1.23	2.42	0.18	0.21
D TOTAL EMPLOYMENT FOR GREY AREAS (1991)	6,400	7,600	46,100	33,000	15,600	248,600	53,900	122,400	322,500
E TOTAL WASTE FOR GREY AREAS (D x C)	12,676	193,188	165,690	201,058	644,884	304,548	130,605	21,593	69,040
F TOTAL WASTE ARISING IN THE REGION (A + E)	56,845	854,093	606,332	793,264	2,707,686	509,377	207,175	34,965	130,309
WEST MIDLANDS									
A TOTAL TONNES OF KNOWN WASTE	1,619	295,281	295,698	602,887	387,974	250,700	27,432	27,400	194,900
B TOTAL EMPLOYMENT FOR WHITE AREAS (1991)	11,000	55,700	131,500	94,500	9,600	204,700	66,300	118,800	304,300
C TONNES PER EMPLOYEE FOR THE REGION (A/B)	0.15	5.30	2.25	6.38	40.41	1.22	0.41	0.23	0.64
D TOTAL EMPLOYMENT FOR GREY AREAS (1991)	21,700	34,700	218,300	84,200	80,200	208,200	31,800	73,200	259,200
E TOTAL WASTE FOR GREY AREAS (D x C)	3,194	183,954	490,881	537,176	3,241,199	254,987	13,157	16,883	166,014
F TOTAL WASTE ARISING IN THE REGION (A + E)	4,813	479,235	786,579	1,140,063	3,629,173	505,687	40,589	44,283	360,914

Table A1.2: Regional Estimates of Waste Arising by SIC Division (WDP Data) (Continued)

		1	2	3	4	5	6	7	8	9
EAST MIDLANDS										
A	TOTAL TONNES OF KNOWN WASTE	63,583	1,152,447	255,460	426,377	400,000	279,878	80,935	9,327	48,955
B	TOTAL EMPLOYMENT FOR WHITE AREAS (1991)	19,200	44,100	129,800	174,600	8,600	171,700	42,800	67,500	211,900
C	TONNES PER EMPLOYEE FOR THE REGION (A/B)	3.31	26.13	1.97	2.44	46.51	1.63	1.89	0.14	0.23
D	TOTAL EMPLOYMENT FOR GREY AREAS (1991)	26,600	14,500	35,300	52,900	53,800	140,300	33,000	55,300	216,700
E	TOTAL WASTE FOR GREY AREAS (D x C)	88,089	378,922	69,474	129,183	2,502,326	228,695	62,403	7,641	50,064
F	TOTAL WASTE ARISING IN THE REGION (A + E)	151,672	1,531,369	324,934	555,560	2,902,326	508,573	143,338	16,968	99,019
YORKSHIRE AND HUMBERSIDE										
A	TOTAL TONNES OF KNOWN WASTE	1,241,000	683,346	555,288	658,893	1,356,700	808,191	88,863	42,172	301,332
B	TOTAL EMPLOYMENT FOR WHITE AREAS (1991)	24,100	48,466	109,545	176,889	51,800	219,000	49,855	108,813	309,200
C	TONNES PER EMPLOYEE FOR THE REGION (A/B)	51.49	14.10	5.07	3.72	26.19	3.69	1.78	0.39	0.97
D	TOTAL EMPLOYMENT FOR GREY AREAS (1991)	27,100	29,828	40,760	68,022	42,200	182,900	43,327	60,773	252,200
E	TOTAL WASTE FOR GREY AREAS (D x C)	1,395,481	420,560	206,614	253,375	1,105,265	674,969	77,227	23,553	245,782
F	TOTAL WASTE ARISING IN THE REGION (A + E)	2,636,481	1,103,906	761,902	912,268	2,461,965	1,483,160	166,090	65,725	547,114
NORTH WEST										
A	TOTAL TONNES OF KNOWN WASTE	82,758	20,993,406	321,348	545,886	139,391	139,391	21,499	62,273	401,629
B	TOTAL EMPLOYMENT FOR WHITE AREAS (1991)	23,100	66,720	127,590	121,090	43,500	189,500	59,866	101,934	279,200
C	TONNES PER EMPLOYEE FOR THE REGION (A/B)	3.58	314.65	2.52	4.51	3.20	0.74	0.36	0.61	1.44
D	TOTAL EMPLOYMENT FOR GREY AREAS (1991)	15,800	35,704	114,748	110,348	104,300	327,000	80,992	137,808	458,400
E	TOTAL WASTE FOR GREY AREAS (D x C)	56,605	11,234,241	289,004	497,460	334,218	240,532	29,086	84,189	659,408
F	TOTAL WASTE ARISING IN THE REGION (A + E)	139,363	32,227,647	610,352	1,043,346	473,609	379,923	50,585	146,462	1,061,037
NORTH										
A	TOTAL TONNES OF KNOWN WASTE	57,595	1,329,145	25,812	49,705	613,000	31,464	7,892	557	2,084
B	TOTAL EMPLOYMENT FOR WHITE AREAS (1991)	3,300	24,800	17,100	15,000	13,900	36,300	9,900	16,400	64,600
C	TONNES PER EMPLOYEE FOR THE REGION (A/B)	17.45	53.59	1.51	3.31	44.10	0.87	0.80	0.03	0.03
D	TOTAL EMPLOYMENT FOR GREY AREAS (1991)	30,600	28,500	96,400	85,400	53,200	183,200	46,200	67,500	280,400
E	TOTAL WASTE FOR GREY AREAS (D x C)	534,063	1,527,445	145,513	282,987	2,346,158	158,794	36,829	2,293	9,046
F	TOTAL WASTE ARISING IN THE REGION (A + E)	591,658	2,856,590	171,325	332,692	2,959,158	190,258	44,721	2,850	11,130
ENGLAND										
A	TOTAL TONNES OF KNOWN WASTE	3,044,648	26,256,700	2,543,723	4,154,175	6,041,674	2,392,892	507,722	337,257	1,487,639
B	TOTAL EMPLOYMENT FOR WHITE AREAS (1991)	131,700	318,936	833,470	876,094	245,800	1,487,500	434,891	804,977	2,128,400
C	TONNES PER EMPLOYEE FOR THE REGION (A/B)	23.12	82.33	3.05	4.74	24.58	1.61	1.17	0.42	0.70
D	TOTAL EMPLOYMENT FOR GREY AREAS (1991)	210,700	244,402	958,877	759,031	591,800	2,646,500	729,369	1,534,331	3,644,000
E	TOTAL WASTE FOR GREY AREAS (D x C)	4,870,974	20,120,620	2,926,461	3,599,097	14,546,227	4,257,337	851,516	642,831	2,546,963
F	TOTAL WASTE ARISING IN ENGLAND (A + E)	7,915,622	46,377,320	5,470,184	7,753,272	20,587,901	6,650,229	1,359,238	980,088	4,034,602
	TOTAL WASTE ARISING IN ENGLAND (SUM OF REGIONS)	9,253,712	42,298,146	5,031,535	7,385,311	24,403,346	5,998,388	1,487,409	992,409	4,039,564

Stage 3: Estimation for Scotland, Wales and Northern Ireland

A1.25 It should be noted that no attempts were made to obtain Waste Disposal Plans from Wales, Scotland or Northern Ireland due to the time and resources required for such an exercise. M.E.L Research holds and regularly updates copies of the English plans and it was felt that these would suffice as a starting point. As the project required data to cover the whole of the United Kingdom, however, estimates had to be made for Scotland, Wales and Northern Ireland. This was done on the basis of employment within these areas.

A1.26 It was originally intended that an average of the tonnes per employee for each SIC Division for each region would be taken as a basis for estimating for Wales, Scotland and Northern Ireland. As the production of an average value for positively skewed distributions is problematic (see section 4.5) and in the event the totals for each SIC Division for England derived from pooling all known data were not markedly different from the totals derived from summing the regional estimates, it was not therefore deemed necessary to take an average figure from the different figures for the regions. Instead, a figure of tonnes of waste arising per employee per annum for the whole of England was calculated by dividing the total waste arising figure for each SIC Division by the employment data for England within each Division. These were then multiplied by employment data at SIC Division level for Wales, Scotland and Northern Ireland to arrive at figures for waste arisings. It should be noted that the results for these areas of the UK were derived from an estimate for England and do not necessarily have any independent validity but are rather a means of estimating for the whole of the UK. Nevertheless, the total for Scotland is of the same order of magnitude as that included in the Hazardous Waste Inspectorate Scotland report for 1991-92 of around 10 million tonnes arising.

A1.27 The results of this procedure are shown in Table A1.3.

Table A1.3: Estimated Quantities of Waste Arising in the UK (WDP data) (tonnes)

| | | SIC DIVISION | | | | | | | |
	1	2	3	4	5	6	7	8	9
A	TONNES OF WASTE PER ANNUM (ENGLAND)	7,915,622	46,377,320	5,470,184	7,753,272	20,587,901	6,650,229	1,359,238	980,088	4,034,602
B	NUMBER OF EMPLOYEES (ENGLAND) (1991)	326,700	556,000	1,799,600	1,616,600	794,100	4,021,100	1,161,500	2,343,900	5,723,600
C	TONNES PER EMPLOYEE (A/B)	24.23	83.41	3.04	4.80	25.93	1.65	1.17	0.42	0.70
D	NUMBER OF EMPLOYEES (SCOTLAND) (1991)	59,300	41,400	158,900	179,200	130,100	411,000	116,200	198,400	680,100
E	NUMBER OF EMPLOYEES (WALES) (1991)	23,700	46,100	87,700	82,100	46,400	200,200	41,200	71,800	335,900
F	NUMBER OF EMPLOYEES (N IRELAND) (1991)	7580	10110	32490	62070	24910	101590	21430	38210	229330
G	TONNES OF WASTE PER ANNUM (SCOTLAND) (C x D)	1,436,781	3,453,275	483,003	859,450	3,372,983	679,725	135,982	82,960	479,407
H	TONNES OF WASTE PER ANNUM (WALES) (C x E)	574,228	3,845,314	266,579	393,755	1,202,970	331,097	48,214	30,023	236,778
I	TONNES OF WASTE PER ANNUM (N IRELAND) (C x F)	183,656	843,300	98,759	297,690	645,819	168,013	25,078	15,977	161,656
J	TONNES OF WASTE PER ANNUM (GB) (A+G+H)	9,926,631	53,675,909	6,219,766	9,006,476	25,163,854	7,661,052	1,543,434	1,093,071	4,750,787
K	TONNES OF WASTE PER ANNUM (UK) (I+J)	10,110,287	54,519,209	6,318,525	9,304,166	25,809,673	7,829,065	1,568,513	1,109,048	4,912,443

Stage 4: Disaggregation to SIC Class

A1.28 Stages 2 and 3 in the statistical procedure produced estimates of industrial and commercial waste arising for the UK by Standard Industrial Classification Division. The data required for the project, however, were to be disaggregated to Standard Industrial Classification Class level (2 digit). A further conversion had therefore to be undertaken to break the Divisional data down to Class level.

A1.29 A ratio estimation method was employed for this purpose, based on the distribution of employment in Great Britain within each SIC Division (Census of Employment 1991). An example of this procedure is shown for SIC Division 7 for Scotland below:

SIC Class	Number of employees in Scotland	% of total
71	12900	6
72	81200	41
74	5200	3
75	4100	2
76	17300	9
77	10900	5
79	67800	34
DIV 7	199400	100

A1.30 In this example, therefore, 6% of the waste arising within Division 7 is attributable to SIC Class 71, 41% to SIC Class 72, 3% to SIC Class 74, and so on.

A1.31 Estimates for England, Wales, Scotland and Northern Ireland were derived in this way; the results are shown in Table A1.4 and A1.5.

DETAILED METHODOLOGY FOR CALCULATING TOTAL WASTE ARISINGS

Table A1.4: Factors to be used in the Disaggregation Procedure to SIC Class (WDP data)

	England		Scotland		Wales		N Ireland		UK	
11	72,200	0.22	2,600	0.04	4,700	0.20	0	0.00	79,500	0.19
12	0	0.00	0	0.00	0	0.00	0	0.00	0	0.00
13	19,000	0.06	30,600	0.52	400	0.02	0	0.00	50,000	0.12
14	12,800	0.04	2,600	0.04	2,100	0.09	0	0.00	17,500	0.04
16	177,400	0.54	21,300	0.36	12,200	0.51	5,750	0.76	216,650	0.52
17	45,300	0.14	2,200	0.04	4,300	0.18	1,830	0.24	53,630	0.13
DIV 1	326,700	1.00	59,300	1.00	23,700	1.00	7,580	1.00	417,280	1.00
21	0	0.00	0	0.00	0	0.00	0	0.00	0	0.00
22	103,700	0.19	7,400	0.18	25,300	0.55	470	0.05	136,870	0.21
23	22,500	0.04	2,300	0.06	1,900	0.04	1,550	0.15	28,250	0.04
24	151,800	0.27	11,400	0.28	6,900	0.15	4,160	0.41	174,260	0.27
25	273,200	0.49	20,300	0.49	12,000	0.26	2,770	0.27	308,270	0.47
26	4,800	0.01	0	0.00	0	0.00	1,160	0.11	5,960	0.01
DIV 2	556,000	1.00	41,400	1.00	46,100	1.00	10,110	1	653,610	1.00
31	251,100	0.14	16,700	0.11	11,000	0.13	1,530	0.05	280,330	0.13
32	596,500	0.33	59,300	0.37	19,800	0.23	8,250	0.25	683,850	0.33
33	57,700	0.03	11,500	0.07	3,000	0.03	110	0.00	72,310	0.03
34	421,700	0.23	40,900	0.26	33,800	0.39	7,430	0.23	503,830	0.24
35	210,300	0.12	3,700	0.02	10,500	0.12	2,740	0.08	227,240	0.11
36	182,400	0.10	23,400	0.15	8,700	0.10	11,280	0.35	225,780	0.11
37	79,900	0.04	3,400	0.02	900	0.01	1,170	0.04	85,370	0.04
DIV 3	1,799,600	1.00	158,900	1.00	87,700	1.00	32,510	1.00	2,078,710	1.00
41,42	434,600	0.27	66,500	0.37	22,800	0.28	19,630	0.32	543,530	0.28
43	144,700	0.09	23,600	0.13	3,400	0.04	9,650	0.16	181,350	0.09
44	14,400	0.01	1,100	0.01	600	0.01	210	0.00	16,310	0.01
45	194,000	0.12	20,300	0.11	10,600	0.13	16,000	0.26	240,900	0.12
46	181,500	0.11	16,200	0.09	11,100	0.14	5,690	0.09	214,490	0.11
47	408,400	0.25	34,500	0.19	16,000	0.19	6,260	0.10	465,160	0.24
48	177,500	0.11	13,200	0.07	12,700	0.15	4,270	0.07	207,670	0.11
49	61,500	0.04	3,800	0.02	4,900	0.06	350	0.01	70,550	0.04
DIV 4	1,616,600	1.00	179,200	1.00	82,100	1.00	62,060	1.00	1,939,960	1.00
50	794,100	1.00	130,100	1.00	46,400	1.00	24,190	1.00	994,790	1.00
DIV 5	794,100	1.00	130,100	1.00	46,400	1.00	24,190	1.00	994,790	1.00
61	786,600	0.20	66,500	0.16	25,900	0.13	19,230	0.19	898,230	0.19
62	15,900	0.00	1,100	0.00	1,500	0.01	170	0.00	18,670	0.00
63	32,300	0.01	800	0.00	200	0.00	290	0.00	33,590	0.01
64,65	2,007,000	0.50	203,300	0.49	101,000	0.50	56,930	0.56	2,368,230	0.50
66	1,014,000	0.25	120,500	0.29	63,300	0.32	21,810	0.21	1,219,610	0.26
67	165,300	0.04	18,800	0.05	8,300	0.04	3,150	0.03	195,550	0.04
DIV 6	4,021,100	1.00	411,000	1.00	200,200	1.00	101,580	1.00	4,733,880	1.00
71	115,300	0.10	12,900	0.11	5,600	0.14	850	0.04	134,650	0.10
72	342,400	0.29	40,600	0.35	16,200	0.39	7,380	0.34	406,580	0.30
74	25,700	0.02	5,200	0.04	1,200	0.03	170	0.01	32,270	0.02
75	66,000	0.06	4,100	0.04	0	0.00	920	0.04	71,020	0.05
76	61,000	0.05	8,600	0.07	3,400	0.08	1,790	0.08	74,790	0.06
77	170,800	0.15	10,900	0.09	0	0.00	2,290	0.11	183,990	0.14
79	380,300	0.33	33,900	0.29	14,800	0.36	8,040	0.38	437,040	0.33
DIV 7	1,161,500	1.00	116,200	1.00	41,200	1.00	21,440	1.00	1,340,340	1.00
81	546,100	0.23	43,400	0.22	17,300	0.24	9,150	0.24	615,950	0.23
82	238,300	0.10	26,600	0.13	6,100	0.08	3,190	0.08	274,190	0.10
83	1,310,000	0.56	100,900	0.51	36,500	0.51	19,050	0.50	1,466,450	0.55
84	105,200	0.04	11,400	0.06	5,900	0.08	2,340	0.06	124,840	0.05
85	144,300	0.06	16,100	0.08	6,000	0.08	4,480	0.12	170,880	0.06
DIV 8	2,343,900	1.00	198,400	1.00	71,800	1.00	38,210	1.00	2,652,310	1.00
91	1,142,600	0.20	140,100	0.21	79,100	0.24	55,110	0.24	1,416,910	0.20
92	388,000	0.07	41,500	0.06	15,400	0.05	6,590	0.03	451,490	0.06
93	1,477,900	0.26	176,300	0.26	82,700	0.25	59,080	0.26	1,795,980	0.26
94	80,400	0.01	7,500	0.01	1,600	0.00	1,090	0.00	90,590	0.01
95	1,266,200	0.22	162,800	0.24	81,000	0.24	53,140	0.23	1,563,140	0.22
96	767,900	0.13	83,300	0.12	44,800	0.13	39,730	0.17	935,730	0.13
97	435,800	0.08	51,600	0.08	24,200	0.07	10,070	0.04	521,670	0.07
98	164,800	0.03	17,000	0.02	7,100	0.02	4,540	0.02	193,440	0.03
DIV 9	5,723,600	1.00	680,100	1.00	335,900	1.00	229,350	1.00	6,968,950	1.00

Table A1.5: Results of the Disaggregation Procedure to SIC Class (WDP Data) (tonnes)

SIC DIVISION	TOTAL ARISING ENGLAND (tonnes)	TOTAL ARISING SCOTLAND (tonnes)	TOTAL ARISING WALES (tonnes)	TOTAL ARISING N. IRELAND (tonnes)	SIC CLASS	TOTAL ARISING ENGLAND (tonnes)	TOTAL ARISING SCOTLAND (tonnes)	TOTAL ARISING WALES (tonnes)	TOTAL ARISING N IRELAND (tonnes)	TOTAL ARISING UK (tonnes)
1	7,915,622	1,436,781	574,228	183,656	11	1,749,336	62,995	113,876	0	1,926,207
					12	0	0	0	0	0
					13	460,351	741,408	9,692	0	1,211,451
					14	310,132	62,995	50,881	0	424,008
					16	4,298,229	516,078	295,594	139,317	5,249,218
					17	1,097,575	53,304	104,185	44,339	1,299,403
2	46,377,320	3,453,275	3,845,314	843,300	21	0	0	0	0	0
					22	8,649,871	617,252	2,110,335	39,204	11,416,662
					23	1,876,780	191,849	158,484	129,289	2,356,402
					24	12,662,009	950,902	575,546	346,996	14,535,453
					25	22,788,280	1,693,273	1,000,949	231,052	25,713,555
					26	400,380	0	0	96,758	497,138
3	5,470,184	483,003	266,579	98,759	31	763,260	50,762	33,436	4,648	852,107
					32	1,813,161	180,252	60,185	25,062	2,078,661
					33	175,389	34,956	9,119	334	219,798
					34	1,281,827	124,322	102,741	22,571	1,531,461
					35	639,242	11,247	31,917	8,324	690,729
					36	554,435	71,128	26,445	34,266	686,275
					37	242,869	10,335	2,736	3,554	259,494
4	7,753,272	859,450	393,755	297,690	41,42	2,084,357	318,937	109,350	94,161	2,606,805
					43	693,986	113,186	16,307	46,289	869,769
					44	69,063	5,276	2,878	1,007	78,224
					45	930,431	97,360	50,838	76,749	1,155,378
					46	870,481	77,696	53,236	27,294	1,028,706
					47	1,958,701	165,463	76,737	30,028	2,230,929
					48	851,296	63,308	60,910	20,482	995,996
					49	294,956	18,225	23,501	1,679	338,361
5	20,587,901	3,372,983	1,202,970	645,819	50	20,587,901	3,372,983	1,202,970	645,819	25,809,673
6	6,650,229	679,725	331,097	168,013	61	1,300,905	109,980	42,834	31,806	1,485,526
					62	26,296	1,819	2,481	281	30,877
					63	53,419	1,323	331	480	55,552
					64,65	3,319,243	336,224	167,037	94,162	3,916,666
					66	1,676,987	199,287	104,688	36,074	2,017,035
					67	273,379	31,092	13,727	5,210	323,408
7	1,359,238	135,982	48,214	25,078	71	134,929	15,096	6,553	994	157,573
					72	400,691	47,512	18,958	8,632	475,794
					74	30,075	6,085	1,404	199	37,764
					75	77,236	4,798	0	1,076	83,110
					76	71,385	10,064	3,979	2,094	87,522
					77	199,878	12,756	0	2,679	215,312
					79	445,044	39,671	17,320	9,404	511,439
8	980,088	82,960	30,023	15,977	81	228,349	18,148	7,234	3,826	257,556
					82	99,644	11,123	2,551	1,334	114,651
					83	547,769	42,191	15,262	7,966	613,188
					84	43,939	4,767	2,467	978	52,201
					85	60,338	6,732	2,509	1,873	71,453
9	4,034,602	479,407	236,778	161,656	91	805,426	98,757	55,758	38,844	998,786
					92	273,504	29,254	10,856	4,645	318,258
					93	1,041,781	124,275	58,296	41,642	1,265,994
					94	56,674	5,287	1,128	768	63,857
					95	892,552	114,759	57,097	37,455	1,101,864
					96	541,298	58,719	31,580	28,003	659,600
					97	307,198	36,373	17,059	7,098	367,728
					98	116,169	11,983	5,005	3,200	136,357

67

Raw Data from Surveys

A1.32 M.E.L Research holds the raw data from three counties' Waste Disposal Plan surveys (West Midlands, Humberside and Norfolk) and data from a survey of commercial firms in Sheffield, carried out on behalf of a consortium comprising the DoE, DTi, FoE and INCPEN. In total, this equates to a database holding information on 2918 firms in the UK representing 2% of all UK employment. As the data are in a raw format, the sources of error can be controlled far more tightly than is possible when using secondary data, such as that contained in the Waste Disposal Plans. In addition, the surveys of commercial waste in Sheffield and the West Midlands were conducted from conception to results by M.E.L Research and the errors are therefore well known. Although the data only relate to three counties and one district in England, it is possible to have much greater confidence in the basic data than those from the Waste Disposal Plans described above.

A1.33 The calculation process involved three stages, as follows:

1. Conversion of data into a compatible format and derivation of a tonnes per employee figure for each firm
2. Production of an average tonnes per employee figure for each SIC Class
3. Estimation for the UK

Stage 1: Data conversion and tonnes per employee per firm calculation

A1.34 Firstly, the data from the various surveys were converted into a compatible format and combined in a database. Each record related to one firm, containing information on the SIC Class, the number of employees and the tonnages of various types of waste generated each year. For each firm it was therefore possible to derive a waste per employee figure. It should be noted that no information was collected by the organisations conducting the surveys on proxy variables other than employment (for example gross output or floor space) such that it was impossible to gross up on anything other than employment. These were then grouped by SIC Class in order to derive an average figure for each Class such that this could be used to estimate waste arisings for the UK.

Stage 2: Production of an average tonnes per employee per SIC Class figure

A1.35 The production of an average waste per employee figure is far from straightforward, however. The frequency distribution of the waste per employee figures shows a highly positive skew with many firms producing a small quantity of waste per employee and a few producing large quantities.

A1.36 M.E.L Research has undertaken extensive research into the statistical problem of deriving an accurate population mean from log normally distributed samples on behalf of the West Midlands Waste Management Coordinating Authority[20]. The straight average value is highly unreliable as different samples can produce markedly different means; for example, if just one firm is included in the sample producing an excessively large amount of waste per employee, the sample mean will overestimate the average while for other samples it may underestimate. An alternative is to use the median as the typical value of waste per employee. While this is a consistent estimator of the population *median*, this is of little use for estimating for the whole population as the median will consistently underestimate the total. There is, however, a technique for deriving the *minimum variance unbiased estimate* of the mean (MVUE mean). The formula used for this statistical procedure requires that, within each sub-sample (in this case SIC Class), measures of the mean and the variance of logarithms of tonnes per employee be produced. As it is not possible to take the log of 0, all tonnes per employee values of nought were excluded (a total of 21 firms). This is not thought to bias the results as it is in any case highly unlikely that any company will produce no waste at all. Having derived all necessary information, the formula[21] was applied to each of the SIC Classes, thereby producing a minimum variance unbiased estimate of the mean tonnes per employee. Table A1.6 shows the results of this stage in the calculation and more detail on the statistical methods used here is available from M.E.L Research's report to the West Midlands Waste Management Coordinating Authority *The West Midlands Industrial Waste Survey*.

A1.37 This procedure can be used for the raw survey data although not for the data from the Waste Disposal Plans (which will have certainly used a normal mean for the grossing-up procedure) as no measure of the variance is given or derivable. The degree of confidence that we would wish to place in the results from the three sources (Waste Disposal Plans, raw survey data and other secondary sources) is discussed in Chapter 5 of this report.

Stage 3: Production of UK estimates

A1.38 Employment data for the UK (Census of Employment 1991) were then applied to the tonnes per employee figures derived in this way to estimate the quantity of industrial and commercial waste arising in the UK.

Table A1.6: Calculating the Minimum Variance Unbiased Estimate of the Mean

SIC CLASS	SAMPLE	MIN	MEDIAN	MEAN	MAX	S.D.	LOGAV	LOGVAR	EXP(H)	TERM 1	TERM 2	TERM 3	MVUE	EXP(2*H)	VAR 1	VAR 2	VAR 3	VAR 4	VAR 5	VAR 6	MVUE VAR	LIMIT
11 TO 14	28	0.05	1.96	8.91	62.01	15.92	0.81884	3.225356	2.267867585	3.52672086	2.55305548	0.001581128	8.35	5.143223382	31.99254376	92.6398682	0.229490442	15.4038173	21.4761834	0.02561553	87.95628611	3.4738454
16	9	0.01	1.49	4.9	19.45	6.44	0.219728	5.634514	1.245737844	3.11961214	3.12488858	0.027171649	7.52	1.551862775	15.54487562	62.2846715	2.166320084	6.80088308	11.9216754	0.18140815	61.09190056	5.1065387
17	2	0	0.25	1.03	2.83	1.57	-0.173009	2.944124	0.841130045	0.61909778	0.07594586	0.003726567	1.54	0.707499752	2.082967	1.02208552	0.200609768		0	0	3.30566229	2.5198246
21	2	0.86	0.95	0.95	0.95	0.13	-0.055801	0.018058	0.945727317	0.00426948	3.21243E-06	9.66835E-10	0.95	0.894400158	0.016151078	4.86094E-05	5.85192E-08		0	0	0.016199746	0.1763986
22	137	0.04	5.85	18.93	344	42.42	1.665704	2.693704	5.289395674	7.0720329	4.65921032	0.000109059	17.02	27.97770659	149.6271209	394.310510	0.036918867	74.2634607	97.1332863	0.00451380	372.5732896	3.2322254
23	2	0.03	0.25	0.25	0.48	0.32	-2.120264	3.843624	0.119999944	0.11530866	0.01846679	0.00118299	0.25	0.014399987	0.055348134	0.03545623	0.009085363		0	0	0.098889733	0.4380276
24	47	0.2	6.87	15.81	120.5	25.34	1.573538	2.934822	4.823684234	6.92772459	4.76748085	0.00099232	16.52	23.26792959	133.6686237	367.949155	0.306344759	65.3813920	88.0313137	0.03584961	348.4755684	5.3369521
25	103	0.12	4.55	14.93	720.6	71.28	1.421373	1.821876	4.142804608	3.73719893	1.65323587	4.5979E-05	9.53	17.16283002	61.92993993	109.584531	0.012190842	30.6613918	26.8615869	0.00147947	114.0022035	2.0620257
26	2	0.55	2.07	2.07	3.59	2.15	0.340158	1.759668	1.40516959	0.61815799	0.04532303	0.001329225	2.07	1.974501576	3.47446724	1.01898480	0.119953833		0	0	4.612990373	2.9766813
31	628	0.02	2.9	14.74	2455.	102.03	1.165323	2.396928	3.206958564	3.83730428	2.28847424	2.30707E-06	9.33	10.28458323	49.22430336	117.424673	0.000473615	24.5728978	29.2626028	5.89067E-05	112.8138903	0.8307254
32	264	0	1.74	4.32	70.01	8.43	0.525989	1.907736	1.692131539	1.60795622	0.75821819	3.42016E-06	4.06	2.863309146	10.88349377	20.5280787	0.000370391	5.42105583	5.09306710	4.57727E-05	20.89777416	0.5514474
33	2	0.06	0.14	0.14	0.23	0.12	-2.141543	0.902812	0.117473442	0.02651410	0.00099738	1.50075E-05	0.14	0.013800009	0.012458814	0.00187466	0.000112831		0	0	0.014446306	0.1665787
34	120	0.02	1.16	3.98	68.28	9.07	0.292616	2.130754	1.339928159	1.41563257	0.73544664	1.76948E-05	3.49	1.795407472	7.587383777	15.7671308	0.001517429	3.76181212	3.87581260	0.00018493	15.71822234	0.7093607
35	89	0.01	3.37	10.14	278.1	32.34	1.16646	2.134862	3.210606949	3.88859462	1.74848641	7.59800E-05	8.35	10.30799698	43.51778186	89.8192420	0.015612415	21.5116308	21.9473735	0.00188577	89.89174657	1.9697947
36	29	0.04	1.74	4.15	36	6.92	0.640182	1.750702	1.89682607	1.60313381	0.63229365	0.000198807	4.13	3.597949141	12.16346408	19.1896173	0.024134556	5.86452732	4.46085173	0.00270499	21.04913194	1.6698373
37	23	0.02	1.85	8.44	110.3	22.83	0.352893	4.663588	1.423178855	3.17427470	3.24497217	0.004217729	7.85	2.025438054	18.07024254	73.8908124	0.384165336	8.62443394	16.8315332	0.04176553	66.84748766	3.3414479
41,42	62	0.01	4.55	20.12	496.9	70.06	1.345002	3.073451	3.838194217	5.80311784	4.24771258	0.000539915	13.89	14.73173485	89.09397345	260.856734	0.132627029	43.8167082	63.0935395	0.01577634	243.1573105	3.8815384
43 TO 45	57	0.02	1.04	5.73	87.53	15.97	0.125491	2.80087	1.133704966	1.55982607	1.03605388	0.000141416	3.73	1.285286949	7.073530273	18.7932708	0.010260723	3.47360861	4.53201884	0.0012151	17.8702193	1.0974470
46	93	0.01	4.99	13.12	337.6	36.47	1.327477	3.3751	3.771515839	2.9618476	5.14362111	0.000324078	15.21	14.22433173	94.98464225	310.387975	0.078225094	46.9761002	75.9192706	0.00946273	282.5460096	3.4163250
47	113	0	1.76	5.95	101.4	14.05	0.665318	2.143708	1.945108968	2.06642262	1.07839418	2.93938E-05	5.09	3.783448896	16.07766872	33.5615071	0.003659143	7.96705905	8.24121749	0.00044525	33.43411317	1.0661339
48	85	0.02	2.72	4.53	31.57	5.98	0.764821	2.037284	2.148600739	2.16291513	1.06334026	4.82693E-05	5.37	4.616523811	18.58904207	36.5552518	0.006637561	9.18387197	8.92251735	0.00060041	37.0437417	1.2939098
49	46	0.06	1.26	2.71	14.29	3.22	0.287103	1.749691	1.33256146	1.14044223	0.46724428	6.04505E-05	2.94	1.775720045	6.078837486	9.96210761	0.00515546	2.97187610	2.38106670	0.00060241	10.69255533	0.9449697
50	27	0.01	1.6	4.2	40	8.05	-0.019659	4.035255	0.980532978	2.01066957	1.61709644	0.001426867	4.61	0.961444921	7.471967485	26.9606810	0.089541747	3.59229206	6.23166628	0.00995028	24.68828162	1.8742159
61	180	0	1.23	6.49	161.1	16.64	0.362241	3.034489	1.436545108	2.16748132	1.61709644	2.48283E-05	5.22	2.063661846	12.4547388	37.1685118	0.002282684	6.19257962	9.18859531	0.00028058	34.24407783	0.8548945
62	8	0.09	5.5	233.39	1700	593.63	2.193494	3.392913	8.966487354	36.8468780	58.8849878	1.047540848	105.75	80.39789546	1321.548266	8447.86397	601.1367528	566.377828	1551.64848	47.3198027	8205.202878	62.770521
64,65	98	0	1.7	7.24	319.4	32.27	0.515641	2.408487	1.674711648	1.99618142	1.16564558	4.72729E-05	4.84	2.804659104	13.37211315	31.2239238	0.005066781	6.61712815	7.64831125	0.00061396	30.34505043	1.0906539
66	37	0.1	1.9	3.33	21.24	4.17	0.604581	1.32694	1.830485075	1.18164836	0.36132601	5.3993E-05	3.37	3.35067561	8.651958798	10.5824301	0.006325338	4.20581330	2.50067069	0.00072659	12.53350366	1.1407525
67	17	0.19	0.79	2.31	10.9	3.18	0.160036	1.344368	1.173553118	0.74244106	0.20875587	0.000137571	2.12	1.377226921	3.485176097	3.91977764	0.010332595	1.63367629	0.86127926	0.00106422	4.919266551	1.0543426
71 TO 79	175	0	0.53	3.61	152.1	14.74	-0.321862	2.738918	0.724798206	0.98690953	0.66426927	9.73451E-06	2.38	0.525332439	2.861241031	7.70337881	0.000451555	1.42239855	1.90377216	5.54768E-05	7.238445195	0.3986315
81 TO 85	201	0	0.39	20.3	2889	204.61	-0.540384	3.411231	0.582536171	0.98863952	0.83061863	1.15169E-06	2.40	0.339534839	2.30367313	7.74184640	0.000429376	1.14607738	1.91615537	5.2871E-05	6.983663289	0.3653420
91 TO 99	191	0	0.46	11.53	1369.	105.81	-0.522616	2.232147	0.592967315	0.65833021	0.36164227	3.63091E-06	1.61	0.351610236	1.561473188	3.43107277	0.000137793	0.77662745	0.84876281	1.69536E-05	3.367276531	0.2602428
ALL	2892	0.01	1.86	11.28712	2889	7576.0	0.612056	2.961433	1.844219218	2.72982157	2.01895037	1.19023E-07	6.59	3.401144525	20.13755767	59.5741932	1.40482E-05	10.0652960	14.8832467	1.75421E-06	54.76322045	0.2697127

LOGAV — Average of the log values
LOGVAR — Variance of the log values
EXP(H) — Exponent of average of the log
TERM 1 — First term of the formula for the mean
TERM 2 — Second term of the formula for the mean
TERM 3 — Third term of the formula for the mean
MVUE MEAN — MVUE of the mean (EXP(H)+TERM1+TERM 2+TERM 3)
EXP(2*H) — Exponent of 2 x log values

VAR 1 — First term of formula for variance
VAR 2 — Second term of the formula for variance
VAR 3 — Third term of the formula for variance
VAR 4 — Fourth term of the formula for variance
VAR 5 — Fifth term of the formula of the variance
VAR 6 — Sixth term of the formula of the variance
MVUE VAR — MVUE for the variance (VAR1+VAR2+VAR3-VAR4+VAR5-VAR6)
LIMIT — 2 x Standard Error of mean

Table A1.7: Estimated Quantities of Waste Arising in the UK (survey data) (tonnes)

SIC CLASS	SAMPLE	MVUE MEAN (tonnes per employee)	LIMIT (tonnes per employee)	UK EMPLOYMENT	UK WASTE ARISINGS (tonnes)	LOWER LIMIT (tonnes)
11 TO 14	28	8.35	3.47	147,000	1,227,336	716,681
16	9	7.52	5.11	216,650	1,628,647	522,315
17	2	1.54	2.52	53,630	82,585	0
21	2	0.95	0.18	0	0	0
22	137	17.02	3.23	136,870	2,329,630	1,887,235
23	2	0.25	0.44	28,250	7,203	0
24	47	16.52	5.34	174,260	2,878,755	1,948,737
25	103	9.53	2.06	308,270	2,938,826	2,303,165
26	2	2.07	2.98	5,960	12,337	0
31	628	9.33	0.83	280,330	2,616,247	2,383,370
32	264	4.06	0.55	683,850	2,775,275	2,398,168
33	2	0.14	0.17	72,310	10,485	0
34	120	3.49	0.71	503,830	1,758,883	1,401,486
35	89	8.35	1.97	227,240	1,896,946	1,449,330
36	29	4.13	1.67	225,780	933,025	556,009
37	23	7.85	3.34	85,370	669,868	384,609
41,42	62	13.89	3.88	543,530	7,549,395	5,439,662
43 TO 45	57	3.73	1.10	438,560	1,635,709	1,154,412
46	93	15.21	3.42	214,490	3,262,746	2,529,978
47	113	5.09	1.07	465,160	2,367,644	1,871,721
48	85	5.37	1.29	207,670	1,116,208	847,502
49	46	2.94	0.94	70,550	207,439	140,771
50	27	4.61	1.87	994,790	4,581,540	2,717,088
61	180	5.22	0.85	898,230	4,689,792	3,921,900
62	8	105.75	62.77	18,670	1,974,276	802,350
64,65	98	4.84	1.09	2,368,230	11,454,148	8,871,229
66	37	3.37	1.14	1,219,610	4,114,371	2,723,098
67	17	2.12	1.05	195,550	415,522	209,345
71 TO 79	175	2.38	0.40	1,340,340	3,184,630	2,650,328
81 TO 85	201	2.40	0.37	2,652,310	6,370,334	5,401,333
91 TO 99	191	1.61	0.26	6,968,950	11,240,522	9,426,903
SUM OF CLASSES	2892			22,055,340	85,930,320	64,658,725

Published results of independent surveys

A1.39 The results of two independent surveys are cited in a report by Aspinwall and Company[13] on the techniques used to determine industrial and commercial waste arisings. They are included as an illustration of the different estimates of tonnes per employee that may be derived from different surveys. As the resulting estimates are so different to other published figures and those derived from the Waste Disposal Plans and survey data, they are included in Appendix 4 for illustrative purposes only.

Data Carried Forward

A1.40 The estimate of total waste arising in the UK derived from the Waste Disposal Plan data is around 121 million tonnes while the estimate derived from the survey data is slightly lower at 85 million tonnes. Both sets will be carried forward to estimate the impact on industry of an increase in landfill price and will be refined in Chapter 5 of the report. Some discussion on the differences between the two data sets is also included in this chapter.

Table A1.8: Comparison of Waste Arisings Estimates Derived from the Two Sources of Data to be Carried Forward

INDUSTRY GROUP	TONNES OF WASTE ARISING PER ANNUM		DIFFERENCE BETWEEN THE TWO DATA SETS (TONNES)
	Survey data	WDP data	
Coal extraction; coke ovens; extraction of oil and gas etc	1,227,366	3,561,666	-2,334,330
Prod and dist of electricity, gas and other forms of energy	1,628,647	5,249,218	-3,620,571
Water supply industry	82,585	1,299,403	-1,216,818
Extraction and preparation of metalliferous mineral ores	MISSING	MISSING	MISSING
Metal manufacturing	2,329,630	11,416,662	-9,087,032
Extraction of minerals not elsewhere specified	7,203	2,356,402	-2,349,199
Manufacture of non-metallic mineral products	2,878,755	14,535,453	-11,656,698
Chemical industry	2,939,826	25,713,555	-22,774,729
Production of man-made fibres	12,337	497,138	-484,801
Manufacture of metal goods not elsewhere specified	2,616,247	852,107	1,764,140
Mechanical engineering	2,775,275	2,078,661	696,614
Manufacture of office machinery & data processing equip.	10,485	219,798	-209,313
Electrical and electronic engineering	1,758,883	1,531,461	227,422
Manufacture of motor vehicles and parts thereof	1,896,946	690,729	1,206,217
Manufacture of other transport equipment	933,025	686,275	246,750
Instrument engineering	669,868	259,494	410,374
Food, drink and tobacco manufacturing industries	7,549,395	2,606,805	4,942,590
Textiles, leather and leather goods, footwear and clothing	1,635,709	2,103,370	-467,661
Timber and wooden furniture industries	3,262,746	1,028,706	2,234,040
Man. of paper and paper products; printing and publishing	2,367,644	2,230,929	136,714
Processing of rubber and plastics	1,116,208	995,996	120,212
Other manufacturing industries	207,439	338,361	-130,922
Construction	4,581,540	25,809,673	-21,228,133
Wholesale distribution	4,689,792	1,485,526	3,204,266
Dealing in scrap and waste materials	1,974,276	30,877	1,943,399
Commission agents	MISSING	55,552	MISSING
Retail distribution	11,454,148	3,916,666	7,537,482
Hotels and catering	4,114,371	2,017,035	2,097,336
Repair of consumer goods and vehicles	415,522	323,408	92,114
Transport and communication	3,184,630	1,568,512	1,616,118
Banking, finance, insurance, business services, leasing	6,370,334	1,109,048	5,261,285
Other services	11,240,522	4,912,443	6,328,079
All economic activities	**85,930,320**	**121,480,928**	**-35,550,608**

APPENDIX 2

COMPARATIVE DATA FROM OTHER
EUROPEAN MEMBER STATES

A2 COMPARATIVE DATA FROM OTHER EUROPEAN MEMBER STATES

Introduction

A2.1 In addition to UK data, information on industrial and commercial waste arising and being disposed of to landfill was requested from the Netherlands and Germany. Both countries conduct national surveys of industrial waste producers through a postal questionnaire on a regular basis. The results are compiled such that they relate the waste to the industry of origin. These data were requested as it was thought that they may help in choosing which set of data to use - Waste Disposal Plans or survey data.

Information used in this project

A2.2 Information was supplied by both Holland and Germany listed according to the national classification of businesses used in these countries. A conversion therefore had to be undertaken into Standard Industrial Classification 1980 format, as follows:

Dutch Business Classification (SBI)		Standard Industrial Classification 1980	
1	Mining and quarrying	11	Mining and quarrying
20/21	Manufacture of food, beverages and tobacco products	41/42	Food, drink and tobacco manufacturing industries
22	Manufacture of textiles	43	Textile industry
23	Manufacture of clothing exc shoes	44,45	Manufacture of leather and leather goods; Footwear and clothing industries
24	Manufacture of leather, footwear and other leather products exc clothing		
25	Manufacture of wood products inc furniture	46	Timber and wooden furniture industries
26	Manufacture of paper and paper products	47	Manufacture of paper and paper products; printing and publishing
27	Printing, publishing and allied industries		
28	Petroleum industry	14	Mineral oil processing
29/30	Chemical industry, manufacture of artificial and synthetic filaments and staple fibres exc glass	25	Chemical industry
31	Manufacture of rubber and plastic products	48	Processing of rubber and plastics
32	Manufacture of building materials, earthenware, glass and glass products	24	Manufacture of non-metallic mineral products
33	Basic metal industry	22	Metal manufacturing
34	Manufacture of fabricated metal products, exc machinery and transport equipment	31	Manufacture of metal goods not elsewhere specified
35	Mechanical engineering	32	Mechanical engineering
36	Electrical engineering	34	Electrical and electronic engineering
37	Manufacture of transport equipment	35,36	Manufacture of motor vehicles and parts thereof; Manufacture of other transport equipment
38	Instrument engineering	37	Instrument engineering
39	Other manufacturing industries	49	Other manufacturing industries
4	Public utilities	16,17	Production and distribution of electricity, gas and other forms of energy; Water supply industry

A2.3 As the table above shows, not all of the business sectors mapped exactly onto the UK Standard Industrial Classification. In these cases, industry sectors have been combined.

German Business Classification	Standard Industrial Classification 1980	
Electricity, gas, steam and water supply	16	Production and distribution of electricity, gas and other forms of energy
	17	Water supply industry
Mining	11	Coal extraction and manufacture of solid fuels
	21	Extraction and preparation of metalliferous ores
Mineral oil industry	13	Extraction of mineral oil and natural gas
	14	Mineral oil processing
Quarrying, extraction, working up of stones and earth	23	Extraction of minerals not elsewhere specified
Iron and steel industry	22	Metal manufacturing
Non-ferrous metal industry and semi-finished products		
Foundries	31	Manufacture of metal goods not elsewhere specified
Manufacture of metal products, rolling stock		
Manufacture of tools and finished metal goods		
Chemical industry	25	Chemical industry
Wood working industry	46	Timber and wooden furniture industries
Pulp, paper and paperboard industries	47	Manufacture of paper and paper products; printing and publishing
Printing and related industries		
Rubber manufacturing industries	48	Processing of rubber and plastics
Plastic products industry		
Mechanical engineering	32	Mechanical engineering
Manufacture of road vehicles; repair of motor vehicles etc	35	Manufacture of motor vehicles and parts thereof
	67	Repair of consumer goods and vehicles
Shipbuilding	36	Manufacture of other transport equipment
Manufacture of aircraft and spacecraft		
Electrical engineering; repair of electrical household goods	34	Electrical and electronic engineering
Manufacture of precision and optical instruments	37	Instrument engineering
Manufacture of office machinery and data processing equipment	33	Manufacture of office machinery and data processing equipment
Musical instruments, toys and fountain pen industries	49	Other manufacturing industry
Fine ceramics industry	24	Manufacture of non-metallic mineral products
Glass and glass products industry		
Leather industry	44	Manufacture of leather and leather goods
Leather products industry		
Textile industry	43	Textile industry
Clothing industry	45	Footwear and clothing industries
Food, beverages and tobacco industries	41/42	Food, drink and tobacco manufacturing industries
Construction	50	Construction

A2.4 The German business classification system draws a distinction between three different broad types of industry groupings - primary and producers goods industries, investment goods producing industries and consumer goods producing industries - with some industries appearing under more than one heading. For example, wood working industries appear under the 'primary and producers goods industry' heading and under the 'consumer goods producing industries' heading. The UK system draws no such distinction so in cases where an industry appears more than once, it has been combined into one heading (for example, 'wood working industries' for the case stated above).

A2.5 Having performed the conversion, it was then possible to derive values of waste arising per employee from the data provided for each industry sector and compare them with the data derived for the UK, both from survey data and Waste Disposal Plans. This comparison is shown in Table A2.1. It should be noted that the Waste Disposal Plan data reflect the disaggregation procedure from SIC Division to SIC Class in that the waste per employee estimates are on Division level.

A2.6 While it is interesting to compare the values from the four different sources, the results from Holland and Germany will not be used in this study as it is unclear to what extent these observed differences are due to real differences in the productivity and waste generation characteristics between UK firms and firms in Holland and Germany. Neither the German data nor the Netherlands data supports either the survey data or the Waste Disposal Plan data. For example, for metal manufacturing, the German estimate would appear to be of the same order of magnitude as the Waste Disposal Plan data while the Netherlands' data would support the survey data. However, this situation is reversed for timber and wooden furniture industries where the German data tends towards the survey data. For this project, therefore, the table is included for illustrative purposes only. Further research into the methods used in Holland and Germany would be required in order to ascertain whether the observed differences are real or due to methodological discrepancies.

Table A2.1: Comparison of the Estimated Tonnes Per Employee Coefficients (WDP data, survey data, European data)

Standard Industrial Classification (1980)		Tonnes generated per employee in Holland	Tonnes generated per employee in Germany	Tonnes generated per employee in the UK (1)	Tonnes generated per employee in the UK (2)
11, 21	Mining	x	53.4	x	x
13, 14	Extraction of mineral oil and gas; mineral oil processing	x	24.525	x	x
16, 17	Public utilities	x	x	9.06	48.46
22	Metal manufacturing	12.4	55.34	17.02	83.41
23	Quarrying	x	46.9	0.25	83.41
24	Manufacture of non-metallic mineral products	13.4	6.29	16.52	83.41
25	Chemical industry	7	15.73	9.53	83.41
31	Manufacture of metal goods not elsewhere specified	1.8	8.75	9.33	3.04
32	Mechanical engineering	0.7	2.76	4.06	3.04
33	Manufacture of office machinery	x	1.17	0.14	3.04
34	Electrical and electronic engineering	0.4	1.57	3.49	3.04
35, 36	Manufacture of motor vehicles and parts and other transport	0.8	3.72	12.48	3.04
37	Instrument engineering	0.3	1.02	7.85	3.04
41, 42	Food, drink and tobacco manufacturing industries	18.4	22.31	13.89	4.80
43, 44, 45	Textile, leather and leather goods industries	1.35	2.4	3.73	4.80
46	Timber and wooden furniture industries	6	22.33	15.21	4.80
47	Man. of paper and paper products; printing & publishing	5.42	22.72	5.09	4.80
48	Processing of rubber and plastic	1.7	3.71	5.37	4.80
49	Other manufacturing industries	0.5	1.45	2.94	4.80
50	Construction	x	99.18	4.61	25.94

(1) Survey data (2) Waste Disposal Plan data x missing data

APPENDIX 3

EXPLANATION OF THE SOURCES OF
DATA INCLUDED IN TABLE 6.1

A3 EXPLANATION OF THE SOURCES OF DATA INCLUDED IN TABLE 6.1

A3.1 **Column 1: Industry Group**
Source: Standard Industrial Classification 1980 (CSO: HMSO)

A3.2 **Column 2: Annual Output Per Annum (£ Million)**
Source: Census of Production 1991 (CSO: HMSO)
The gross output for SIC Class 21 (Extraction and preparation of metalliferous ores) is missing from the Census of Production because there are insufficient examples of firms in this sector to ensure that individual firms can not be identified. SIC Class 50 (Construction) and Classes 61- 98 (Commerce) are missing as they are not covered by the Census of Production or any equivalent.

A3.3 **Columns 3 & 4: Cost of a £5 Increase in Landfill Price (£ million)**
Source: The results presented in columns 4 & 5 in Table 5.1 multiplied by £5 and converted into £ millions.
SIC Class 21 is missing because no employment data are available due to a confidentiality issue. SIC Class 63 is missing because no firms of this type were surveyed.

A3.4 **Columns 5 & 6: Cost of Price Increase as Percentage of Gross Output**
Source: Columns 4 and 5 as a percentage of column 2.
SIC Class 63 is missing because no firms of this type were surveyed. SIC Class 21 is missing from the Census of Production and the Census of Employment because there are insufficient examples of firms in this sector to ensure that individual firms can not be identified. SIC Class 50 (Construction) and Classes 61- 98 (Commerce) are missing as they are not covered by the Census of Production or any equivalent.

APPENDIX 4

PUBLISHED RESULTS OF
OTHER INDEPENDENT SURVEYS
(ADER AND TRON)

A4 PUBLISHED RESULTS OF OTHER INDEPENDENT SURVEYS

A4.1 The results of two independent surveys are cited in a report by Aspinwall and Company[13] on the techniques used to determine industrial and commercial waste arisings. They are included as an illustration of the different estimates of tonnes per employee that may be derived from different surveys.

A4.2 The first of these sources is an unpublished Warren Spring Laboratory report by A R Tron dating from 1978[11]. The aim of the study was to estimate the recovery potential of industrial and commercial waste. Data were collected through surveys of industry and commerce in various parts of England and then grossed up using employment data (tonnes per employee) for Great Britain.

A4.3 The second source is a 1983 report by Ader and Buck on behalf of ETSU (Energy Technology Support Unit)[12]. The aim of the study was to provide a system for mapping industrial waste arisings such that potential users of waste derived fuel could be identified. Data were compiled from seven Waste Disposal Plans (Buckinghamshire, Cleveland, Kent, Merseyside, Oxfordshire, Staffordshire and Suffolk). Again, employment data were used as a basis for estimating the national picture.

A4.4 A comparison of the tonnes per employee factors is made by Aspinwall and Company. However, the industrial breakdown is in 1968 SIC format and for the purposes of this study the total tonnages derived from the factors had to be converted into 1980 SIC format. The methodology adopted for this procedure was identical to that used for the Waste Disposal Plans (Appendix 1 of this report).

A4.5 The results of this disaggregation are shown in Table A4.1. The low figure obtained in the Tron study is partly, although not wholly, attributable to the date of the work (1978) as Aspinwall and Company point out in their review. However, even the higher Ader and Buck figure is nowhere near published totals of upwards of 100 million tonnes. While it is interesting to compare the results of these studies with the figures obtained from survey data and Waste Disposal Plans (table 4.9), they could not be used with any degree of confidence for this project as they are so different from official figures and the others obtained through this study. For this report, survey data and data from Waste Disposal Plans have therefore been used to provide two independent estimates of the costs of the proposed landfill levy.

Table A4.1: Comparison of the Results of Waste Arisings
(WDP Data, Survey Data, Ader and Tron)

SIC CLASS	TRON	ADER	SURVEY DATA	WDP DATA
11 TO 14	175,988	118,045	1,227,336	3,561,666
16	251,292	168,556	1,628,647	5,249,218
17	61,721	41,400	82,585	1,299,403
21	986	2,320	MISSING	MISSING
22	149,465	351,570	2,329,630	11,416,662
23	29,257	68,819	7,203	2,356,402
24	186,393	438,432	2,878,755	14,535,453
25	334,762	787,425	2,938,826	25,713,555
26	6,136	14,434	12,337	497,138
31	154,102	160,369	2,616,247	852,107
32	373,426	388,614	2,775,275	2,078,661
33	39,907	41,530	10,485	219,798
34	274,376	285,536	1,758,883	1,531,461
35	124,088	129,135	1,896,946	690,729
36	118,561	123,383	933,025	686,275
37	46,540	48,433	669,868	259,494
41,42	181,338	424,889	7,549,395	2,606,805
43 TO 45	142,848	334,705	1,635,709	2,103,370
46	72,272	169,339	3,262,746	1,028,706
47	158,840	372,174	2,367,644	2,230,929
48	70,403	164,960	1,116,208	995,996
49	24,298	56,933	207,439	338,361
50	696,000	593,000	4,581,540	25,809,673
61	72,676	719,356	4,689,792	1,485,526
62	1,530	15,140	1,974,276	30,877
63	2,753	27,252	MISSING	55,552
64,65	191,099	1,891,521	11,454,148	3,916,666
66	99,034	980,255	4,114,371	2,017,035
67	15,908	157,456	415,522	323,408
71 TO 79	617,000	1,120,000	3,184,630	1,568,512
81 TO 85	290,050	650,690	6,370,334	1,109,048
91 TO 99	448,950	2,097,330	11,240,522	4,912,443
ALL	5,412,000	12,943,000	85,930,320	121,480,928

Printed in the United Kingdom for HMSO
Dd300871 2/95 C9 G3397 10170